If These WALLS Could TALK:

PHILADELPHIA PHILLIES

Stories from the
Philadelphia Phillies Dugout,
Locker Room, and Press Box

Larry Shenk

TRIUMPH
BOOKS

Library of Congress Cataloging-in-Publication Data

Shenk, Larry.
  If these walls could talk, Philadelphia Phillies : stories from the Philadelphia Phillies dugout, locker room, and press box / Larry Shenk.
     pages cm
  ISBN 978-1-60078-910-6 (pbk.)
  1. Philadelphia Phillies (Baseball team)—History. 2. Philadelphia Phillies (Baseball team)—Anecdotes. I. Title.
  GV875.P45S53 2014
  796.357'640974811—dc23

                                                                           2013040331

This book is available in quantity at special discounts for your group or organization. For further information, contact:

  Triumph Books LLC
  814 North Franklin Street
  Chicago, Illinois 60610
  (312) 337–0747
  www.triumphbooks.com

Printed in U.S.A.

ISBN: 978-1-60078-910-6

Design by Amy Carter

Photos courtesy of The Phillies

This book is dedicated to the following who mean so much to me…

To Maebelle and Lester Shenk, my parents, and my sisters, Corinne Krall and Rochelle Ebling. Know Mom is looking down on all of us.

To my wife, Julie, for always being there for me. You are everything: wife, mother, grandmother. I'm eternally grateful and I love you.

To our children, Debi Mosel and Andy. God truly blessed us with awesome children. We're so proud of you.

Because of baseball's long hours, Julie, Debi, and Andy sacrificed a lot while I lived my dream. I'm forever indebted for their understanding, support, and love. This book wouldn't have been possible without their encouragement.

To Michael Mosel and Renee Acres Shenk, two wonderful additions to our family.

To two precious grandchildren, Audrey and Tyler Shenk, yet another blessing. With their arrival, Julie and I happily became Mimi and Baba.

Baseball is a great game. Important, yes, but shallow when compared to families filled with love.

CONTENTS

FOREWORD

Philadelphia is a tough town.

After 25 years in a Phillies uniform—12 as a player, nine-plus as a coach, and four as the manager—I feel I can say that. The fans are tough, the media is tough, and because of that, the players have to be tough. So can you imagine being the person who has to bring them all together? For 44 years—including all 25 of mine—Larry Shenk was that man for the Phillies. Whether it was waiting up well past midnight for Paul Owens to complete a trade or calming down Dallas Green after a big loss or reminding the media that Steve Carlton wouldn't be speaking to reporters, Larry was in the middle of everything. And he was someone we, as players, all relied on and trusted. Trust is a hard thing to come by in baseball, but the "Baron" had ours.

When Larry would ask us to do interviews, it was hard for guys to say no, mainly out of respect. He'd been with the Phillies so long and had a very low-key demeanor, which made it difficult for people to say no to him. That's not to say that we always said yes—because we didn't—but even through the most aggravating circumstances, I can't recall seeing Larry get mad at a player. I have to imagine I would have, if I had been in his shoes.

Larry was unique in that he would understand both the players' point of view and the media's. He knew how hard a 162-game schedule was (not to mention over a month of spring training and possible playoffs) and the toll it took on players both mentally and physically. He also knew that the media was there to do a job, and that white space had to be filled somehow, so players needed to talk. It is a very delicate balance, but it was one that Larry handled with class and dignity.

Timing was everything with Larry. He wanted Phillies players under his watch to be accountable for what happened on the field. That was a big thing with him. Every year in spring training, he would say to us, "The training room should not be a hideout." And he was right.

Larry was very good at preparing players—especially me—for not just what questions we might get asked, but also how to best answer them. He would tell me, "Bo, if you have a bad game, you get in front of that microphone and say, 'I messed up. I should have made that play' as opposed to 'That ball took a bad hop.'" He would often remind us that if we were up front with the media and admitted to mistakes, we'd never have any problem with the tough crowd. And he was right.

As respected as Larry was in Philadelphia and around the baseball world, there is no doubt he did a better job than people think when you consider the players he had to deal with. When I think back to that 1980 team—when Larry was in his prime as a PR guy—we had guys who, if they had a bad game, wouldn't talk. Whether it was Mike Schmidt, Greg Luzinski, or even me. Sometimes, a player just can't be convinced to do something he may know is right. It was Larry's job to then go out and deal with the media while we would wait for them to leave. He was a team player in that regard and he had our backs, even if he didn't agree with us.

Larry's longevity is amazing. When you're in baseball a long time, it's hard not to have people talk about you in a negative way. I can honestly say in all my years in the game—and having now worked on both sides of the equation with ESPN, MLB Network, and Sirius/XM Radio—I never heard anyone say a bad word about him. No one ever badmouthed him, and I guess that goes back to his professionalism and how he carried himself. With the exception of Lefty (Steve Carlton), I can't remember one player who consistently refused to do what Larry asked. He had a way about him. And with regard to those who worked under him, he would never put anyone in a situation where they felt uncomfortable. In other words he didn't ask others to get a player that he knew might be difficult. He'd do it himself.

I've always told people that Philly is right there with New York and Boston as the toughest media cities. There's no way I would ever have wanted to do Larry's job. It's like being a utility player. When you go into the game in the eighth inning for defense, it's a no-win situation. You better catch everything because if you make an error, you're a bum. You can sit on the bench for eight innings and be ice cold, and everyone knows you're going in for defense. It's a no-win situation just like with the media. If a player speaks, it's because he's supposed to. If he doesn't, then people think the PR person isn't doing his or her job well.

My final time with Larry was when I managed the Phillies for four years. The manager deals with the PR person more than anyone else in the organization. He respected the job I had to do as manager. He knew my time was limited and he worked around that. I always felt like Larry put himself in a player's position, even though he didn't play. I think he weighed both sides of the coin in every situation.

In baseball, a lot of times you will hear the expression: "He's a player's manager." Well, Larry Shenk was a player's PR guy.

—*Larry Bowa*

INTRODUCTION

A s a small-town kid growing up a couple of hours from the big city of Philadelphia, my dream was to work for the Phillies, however unlikely that would be. A journey of rejections was overcome, but in 1963, my dream came true.

Notes, quotes, and anecdotes from 50 years in the game filled a mental notebook, prompting a book, which you are about to read. Hey, you might even fall asleep reading this epic, but that's okay. Don't tell anyone, but I fell asleep a few times while writing this book.

You'll read about a journey that took many turns and a rookie season that ended with one of the game's greatest collapses. Plans for a rare Philadelphia World Series came to a bitter end. Fans had to wait 16 more years for the Fall Classic, one that became the greatest moment in the franchise's 97-year history.

The book is filled with stories from the field, clubhouse, and front office; spring training, championship seasons, and jewel events such as All-Star Games and World Series. Those who wore the red pinstripe uniforms offer their many memories down through the years. There's a history of uniform numbers worn by the Phillies and stories behind those numbers.

There's my first encounter with the great Howard Cosell and an unusual request from the famous broadcaster, a story that will make you chuckle. There are behind-the-scenes insights into Phillies general managers, managers, and players, including Hall of Famers Richie Ashburn, Robin Roberts, Mike Schmidt, Jim Bunning, and Steve Carlton. Learn the thought process behind the emotional closing ceremonies of Veterans Stadium and the opening of Citizens Bank Park.

Hope you enjoy being taken into the Phillies' inner sanctum.

Cheers.

CHAPTER 1
MEN IN PINSTRIPES

More than 1,900 players have worn our uniform since the inaugural game in 1883. No, I wasn't around then and I didn't know all 1,900. I do know that 508 played for us at Veterans Stadium and I was around for three of our homes. Alphabetically the players stretched from Kyle Abbott to Jon Zuber.

Dick Allen

The first time I ever saw Dick Allen was at the Hershey Arena. He was the point guard on the Wampum (Pennsylvania) High School basketball team that reached the state championship three consecutive years. As a sophomore and senior at Wampum, he won the state title. But his ability to hit a baseball overshadowed his hoop skills. Baseball scouts began following Allen as a junior. Scouts in those days doubled as salesmen, and Dick's mother, Era Allen, served as her son's negotiator. She was comfortable with the 66-year-old Phillies scout, John Ogden. Upon graduating from school in 1960, Allen signed a pro baseball contract that included a $60,000 bonus. Allen was a gifted athlete, strong and quick. His instinct on how to play baseball was exceptional, and he was driven to win.

Four years after graduating, he went to spring training and was put at third base, a new position. He had some kind of a rookie season, earning Rookie of the Year honors. Swinging a 42-ounce bat, he could punish the baseball. His titanic home runs at Connie Mack Stadium are legendary. On May 29, 1965, Allen hit a monster home run over the Coca-Cola sign atop the left-field roof in the first inning against the Chicago Cubs' Larry Jackson. Sandy Grady, the columnist I idolized, was at the game. He asked how far the ball had traveled. So he and I left the park and tried to figure out the distance. A man sitting on his porch showed us where the ball had landed. We used our gait to measure length and then estimated the depth of the left-field stands and the distance from home plate. We finally came up with 529 feet. Two years later he became the first player to hit a home run over the center-field fence between the stands and the flagpole at Connie Mack Stadium since the fence was raised to 32 feet in 1934. The homer came off Nellie Briles in a 4–3 win against St. Louis.

Paul Owens, Dick Allen, Ruly Carpenter, and Danny Ozark attend the press conference announcing the return of the slugger to the Phillies in 1975.

Since I didn't travel often in the early years, watching the games on television became the routine. When Allen was due to bat, I didn't dare raid the fridge. I didn't want to risk missing something special. Every game was recorded in a stat book. We took down the game, at-bats, runs, hits, doubles, triples, etc. for hitters. He was one of the few players that always had something else posted in his line other than a game number. Granted, that included strikeouts, too. His Phillies years were sprinkled with controversy. He became a target of the boo birds and wanted out of Philadelphia. In his autobiography, *Crash*, he admitted, "I always was rebellious. I liked doing things my own way." He left the Phillies and played on three other teams.

In early May of 1975, Paul Owens called me into his office and asked, "What do you think would be the fan and media reaction if we brought Dick Allen back?" I couldn't answer right away because I was stunned. Owens wanted a veteran bat between Mike Schmidt and Greg Luzinski. I said I thought the fans would welcome him back, but I wasn't sure about the media. Allen and the media were like oil and water.

We ended up bringing him back and had a press conference in the Veterans Stadium Press Club on May 7. The room was packed. Afterward we went to the field for some photo ops. He was a slugger, and his bat was needed. He took some swings while the cameras clicked. That swing was memorable, pure, and unmistakable. It belonged to Allen. Ten years after his 529-foot home run, No. 15 returned to the Phillies. Seven days after the press conference, he singled in his first at-bat and drew a standing ovation. It was a night I'll never forget.

We were both rookies in 1964. Now we're both graying old-timers. He is a regular at alumni weekends. The fans love him, and his former teammates love him. His laugh can be heard often all weekend. He truly is a Phillies legend.

Larry Andersen

At age 30 he was on our 1983 National League champions, a virtual kid on the Wheeze Kids. At age 40 he was on our 1993 National League champions, the senior citizen of that wacky bunch. So he goes down as our only player to appear in both of those World Series. Although he fit in with both teams, he was more suited for the '93 team of misfits and rejects. No. 47 was a tough reliever with a nasty slider, but he was also adept at keeping the clubhouse loose with masks, wigs, fake teeth, colored hair, etc.

L.A. always had room for fans. He visited children and adults in the hospital without fanfare. He was more than willing to meet fans that had special needs at the ballpark. His popularity carried over to the broadcast booth where he's been a fixture since 1998, adding inside knowledge and humor. During a game broadcast, Scott Franzke was talking about a certain major league umpire. "He has a law degree, L.A.," Franzke said. "[He] passed the bar last off-season. Andersen retorted, "I never passed a bar." During the 2013 season, Andersen said out of the blue, "Scott, I'm going to start a Please Smell Museum for Dogs." He also said, "I was going to ask Dallas Green to autograph his book but was afraid he would ruin my Kindle."

He's also one of the leading pranksters. The television broadcasters have a shirt dress code for each telecast. In early September of 2013, Gary Matthews didn't get the message during the day that a certain sweater was to be worn that night. All broadcasters do their pregame work in a room behind the broadcast booths at Citizens Bank Park. Matthews learned of the change, headed for the Majestic Clubhouse store, and purchased the size XL sweater. Upon returning to the broadcaster's workroom, he left the room and made the mistake of leaving the sweater at his station. Meanwhile, Chris Wheeler's size M is hanging on a hanger, and he's not in the room either. Andersen took Matthews' XL out of the plastic bag and replaced it with Wheeler's medium-sized sweater. Wheeler returned, put on the XL, didn't think anything of it, and headed for the booth and the first three innings. Matthews' time on the air is the fourth through the sixth innings. So just before the fourth, he grabs the plastic bag, pulls out the sweater, and can hardly get it on, let alone zip it. Matthews gets angry with himself for buying the wrong size. The radio booth is adjacent to the TV booth, and Andersen couldn't wait to see Matthews. Andersen cracked up watching Matthews in the booth with the tiny sweater.

Larry Bowa

What do Gavvy Cravath, Hans Lobert, Ryne Sandberg, and Larry Bowa have in common? They were the only ones to play, coach, and manage the Phillies (not counting interim managers). What nobody has in common with Larry is that he was scouted on a bed sheet. The first ever summer draft took place in 1965, and Bowa, a skinny shortstop from Sacramento, California, wasn't selected, even though 824 amateur players were.

Our scout, the late Eddie Bockman, had seen Bowa play at various levels of amateur baseball in the San Francisco Bay area. He knew Bowa had basic baseball tools, knew he had heart, knew he was a competitor, knew he had a temper, and thought it worthy of bringing Owens (director of the farm system then) into the picture.

During the 1965 World Series between the Los Angeles Dodgers and Minnesota Twins, Bockman and Owens met in the latter's hotel suite in Los

Angeles. Bockman told Owens he had some eight-millimeter film of a young infielder and wanted him to see the home movie. They did not have a screen, so Owens took the sheet off his bed, and the two of them scotch taped it to the wall. Even with the film slightly out of focus, Owens could tell that Bowa had three tools: he could run, field, and throw. "His hitting didn't look very pretty," Owens said at the time. But Owens had moved from scouting to the front office a few weeks before that first draft and knew the system lacked middle infielders. When he asked him how much it would take to sign Bowa, Bockman replied, "I believe I can get him for $1,000, would like to kick in a couple hundred more, you know, for shoes and a new glove." Bowa signed for $1,200 on October 12, 1965.

Bockman's scouting report that day: "The past three months Larry has shown consistent progress. He had been inconsistent, and this could have been because of his temperament. He used to have a distinct quick temper, but he's controlled this, and his progress has been steady. He has a major league arm for a shortstop. His glove is getting better, due to the improvement in his range. He's had a problem with the bat but has picked up some improvement. Larry runs well and has good judgment on the bases. He has great desire. Cannot sit around, has to be doing something all the time. He has some leadership in the field. Keep him playing, he could be there in four years, maybe less."

"Bo" made his pro debut in Spartanburg, South Carolina, in 1966 but was ready to quit after going 0–4 with four strikeouts in his first game. He was a victim of a young flamethrower named Nolan Ryan. His first year in our big league camp in Clearwater, Florida, was 1967. He wore No. 53. I remember manager Gene Mauch saying, "I can see him run, can see him catch the ball, can see him throw. When he hits, I don't hear anything."

Bockman said Bowa could reach the majors in four years, maybe less. Bowa made it in four years. A right-handed batter, he began switch-hitting in 1969. The next year he was in the majors, and if it hadn't been for manager Frank Lucchesi, Bowa may not have lasted very long. Off to a slow start as a rookie, Lucchesi stuck with Bowa, who finished his career with a .260 average and 2,191 hits. Bowa was eliminated on the first Hall of Fame ballot because of a low number of votes. To me that is a crime. But that's another story. His career ended as the greatest shortstop in Phillies history…until Jimmy Rollins came along.

Did Bowa have a temper? Well, he's the only player I know who received a plumbing bill from the club. It seems that the porcelain toilet in a restroom behind the Vet dugout got destroyed by Bowa's bat one time. He didn't take failure lightly. In our clubhouse I once made a casual remark, "This team's too tense." Bowa heard me and barked, "WHAT DO YOU MEAN TENSE?" He was an ultracompetitive battler who was scrappy, chirpy, and feisty. He had verbal run-ins with his manager, Green, in 1980, had his own radio talk show in which he didn't hold back opinions, got on the fans at times, but on the field, he was driven to excel. His glove seemed to be made out of gold.

Davey Concepcion was a brilliant shortstop with the Cincinnati Reds during much of Bowa's career. Bowa used to needle him, "Is your name Elmer? I keep seeing E-Concepcion in the box score." Bowa could chirp and agitate his own team, too. He was in constant motion. Bockman said he "has to be doing something all the time." Bowa was chirping in the clubhouse, and Steve Carlton had enough. Lefty walked up to Bowa, put his strong hand around his neck, and squeezed. He didn't say a word, but the message came through. Jim Kaat pitched for the Phillies for a few years and paid Bowa the highest compliment. "Leading 1–0 with two out in the top of the ninth and a runner on third, I wanted the ball hit to Bowa," Kaat said. "He was automatic."

You want to talk about a competitor. During Game 1 of the 1980 World Series, the Kansas City Royals led 4–0 with the Phillies coming to bat with one out in the bottom of the third inning. Bowa started things off with a single. He then stole second—not exactly your textbook play when down by four. That steal sparked a five-run inning, and we went on to win 7–6. When Tug McGraw ended the series with a strikeout, the players rushed to McGraw. I can still see Bowa leaping like a kangaroo on his way to join the delirious pile of happy Phillies.

During that series Bowa started seven double plays, a World Series record that still stands. Following the emotional World Series parade, Bowa said, "All those fans, all in red, entire families, generations of Phillies fans, tears rolling down their faces, those memories will stick with me the rest of my life. To me Philadelphia is the greatest place in the world to play, and an even better place to win."

7

After his playing career, he came back to coach and may have been base-ball's best third-base coach. In later years Bowa coached for Joe Torre with the New York Yankees and Los Angeles Dodgers. When Torre was named man-ager of the USA team in the 2013 World Baseball Classic, he named Bowa his bench coach. On TV he could be seen chewing sunflower seeds constantly while not missing a trick on the field.

While he and fellow Sacramento buddy, John Vukovich, were coaches with us, they shared a high-rise condo on Sand Key Beach one spring. "Bowa always grabbed the TV remote first. The longest I saw a show was 10 seconds," Vukovich said, laughing.

When Ed Wade was running the team, he interviewed many candi-dates before settling on Bowa as manager in 2001. Bringing back Bowa to the Phillies was what we needed. He provided credibility, a known winner who bled Phillies red. Most of the new manager press conferences are held at the ballpark. This time I wanted to do something different. We were welcoming him back to Philadelphia. The top floor of Loews Hotel had the perfect loca-tion, a panoramic view of the city. The luncheon/press conference drew a large media crowd. It was great having No. 10 back in his No. 10 pinstriped jersey.

Three years later Wade made a change, a very difficult one, and decided to remove Bowa as manager. I was told to go to Bowa's office at Citizens Bank Park to see how he wanted to handle the media. Bowa grabbed a yellow tablet, wrote his comments, handed it to me, and said that would be it. He wrote: "I want to thank the Phillies organization for the opportunity to manage. I wish them the best of luck in the coming years." He was miffed as generally is the case with any manager being let go.

Bowa has the distinction of playing in the last game at Connie Mack Stadium and in the first one at Veterans Stadium. (He recorded the first hit there.) Then he managed the last game at the Vet and the first game at Citizens Bank Park. A kid who was cut from his high school team wound up wearing a Phillies uniform for 26 years, the longest in our history. A year behind him came his buddy, Vuk. Two Sacramento natives became fixtures in Philadelphia.

Darren Daulton

Not much attention was paid to the 1980 Amateur Draft in June. Philadelphia's focus was on the Phillies' road to their first world championship. In the 25th round (629th overall selection), the Phillies selected Darren Arthur Daulton, a 170-pound catcher out of Arkansas City, Kansas. He was the fourth catcher we selected that day after Lebo Powell (first round), Doug Maggio (third round), and Jerome Kovar (10th). All three signed professionally but never got beyond three years of minor league baseball. Darren, or Dutch, or Bubba, as he was called, made it big time. The only other player we selected in that draft who had a big league career of significance was shortstop Steve Jeltz.

Dutch was the greatest team leader I've ever seen. Jim Fregosi trusted him to run the clubhouse, patting guys on the back or reaming them out. He'd challenge anyone and was the general on the field. Vukovich said, "I played with better players. I've coached better players. But in 32 years I never saw a bigger leader. For me he set the standard of being a man."

"There was no one else who could even come close [as a leader]," John Kruk said. "But he did it the right way. He would pull people aside one on one. It was always private and very calm and casual. I heard him tell guys on our team, 'If you don't straighten out and start doing things the right way, I'm going to kick your [butt].' And it got straightened out."

Although Daulton didn't get a ring with the Phillies, he did as a member of the 1997 Florida Marlins. He was a veteran whose skills were on the downward trend, but the Marlins wanted him for his leadership in the clubhouse. Al Leiter and Daulton were driving together to the Marlins park the second day Daulton was with the club. He told Leiter he was going to call a team meeting because after one game with the Marlins he saw some things he didn't like. He commanded that kind of respect.

Fregosi pinch hit for Daulton in Pittsburgh a couple of years earlier. After the game Daulton went to Fregosi's office. "He was really pissed and wanted to know why I lifted him," Fregosi said. "I told him, 'You know all those long home runs you hit that go foul. Well, they don't count.' Next day me and (hitting coach) Denis Menke worked with Dutch, and he eventually became a tough out." He had unusual numbers in '93—131 hits, 105 RBIs, 117 walks, and 111 strikeouts.

We swept the second-place St. Louis Cardinals in three games (10–7, 14–6, 6–4) at home in late July to take a seven-game lead. I was in the clubhouse as the players came off the field. Daulton spoke up immediately, "Hey, guys. No popping off to the media. There's a long way to go." His leadership and competitiveness qualities are legendary. So was his toughness. Daulton battled through nine knee surgeries, a fractured right clavicle, a broken right hand, and an incomplete tear of his left rotator cuff. When he was called out on strikes to end one game, he went to the video room to see the pitch which was not a strike. He was so angry he tried to put his right fist through a concrete wall—thus the broken right hand. Daulton had a temper, too.

After games he'd head for the trainer's room before the shower or before a bite to eat. Ice packs were put on each knee for 10 to 12 minutes. It was a routine he needed so that he could get on the field the next day. In my experience there are three people who can walk in a room and gain immediate respect—Daulton, Fregosi, and Green. There's a certain presence about them.

Fast forward to 2013. Daulton stopped by Citizens Bank Park to sign some baseballs and meet some Toyota sponsors for Debbie Nocito, the manager of client services and alumni relations, on June 4. He spent recent summers in Philadelphia, hosting a radio talk show, "Talking Baseball With Dutch," on *97.5 The Fanatic*. He was also a spokesman for Yuengling Brewery, America's oldest brewery. His home was in Clearwater.

A month later he underwent a long and complicated surgery at Jefferson University Hospital to remove two brain tumors that turned out to be malignant. The shocking news didn't deter Daulton, who proclaimed, "Right on; Fight on," typical of his toughness. Equally shocking and sad is that Daulton was the fifth Phillies alumnus to be diagnosed with brain tumors. The others were: Johnny Oates, Ken Brett, McGraw, and Vukovich. I don't know if any two people had more respect for each other than Vuk and Dutch.

The outpouring of love and support from Daulton's friends, Phillies family, 97.5 family, and thousands of fans sincerely touched this tough person. There's a great deal of passion in the Phillies Nation. We've seen that over and over.

A month after brain tumor surgery, Darren Daulton returns to Citizens Bank Park and receives three standing ovations during the 2013 Alumni Weekend festivities.

About a month after surgery, Daulton was able to attend our alumni weekend in which we saluted the 1993 league championship club. His teammates were all shocked at the disturbing news. Many came for the weekend and were so excited that Daulton was able to be there. The first time they saw him turned into a hug-a-thon. The word "love" was spoken often. It was obvious the respect they had for him. Daulton drew standing ovations each of the three days he was introduced on the field. It brought tears to my eyes and a lump in my throat. The ovations were the fans' way of saying how much they loved him.

On a personal note, Daulton is one of my favorite people. He respected my role and that of my staff. He was the go-to person in 1993 and was always willing to cooperate. My wife, Julie, did his fan mail, and he treated her like a queen each year. In 2011 Julie was in a rehab facility following one of her numerous knee surgeries. Darren made a point to visit her and bring a huge bouquet of flowers. He holds a special place in our hearts.

Jay Johnstone

I wouldn't call him a flake, but it's close. He was entertaining. Away from the ballpark, he was a hustler, always looking for a deal. He always carried a stack of business cards with him. Johnstone stayed at the Holiday Inn near the Vet one season. When you live in a hotel, all phone calls are costly. So he would come to the Vet early in the afternoon, find an empty desk in the PR or community relations office and make his local and long distance calls. I kidded that he could come to my house in Delaware and make his 302 area code calls there for no charge.

But if you needed a player to meet a fan, you could count on Johnstone. He was willing to join our wacky promotions. He even smashed watermelons with a baseball bat while blindfolded as part of a pregame promotion. He fell on his butt, which added to the amusement. When we had Old-Timers Games, he would stuff a pillow or two inside his baseball jersey, turn his cap sideways, and walk bowlegged onto the field. Photographers loved him and so did the fans.

One year Johnstone was battling for the league lead in doubles. He "ran" a triple into a double, and that didn't set well with Danny Ozark. The next day

Ozark called a clubhouse meeting and aired out Johnstone. The only problem was that Johnstone wasn't in the clubhouse. He was in the dugout doing an interview I had arranged. Ozark and I often laughed about that.

Tommy Lasorda

Why is Lasorda in a book about the Phillies, you might ask? Well, he was one of us at one time. In 1945 the Phillies signed him as a left-handed pitcher out of Norristown High School. While pitching for the Phillies minor league club in Schenectady, New York, in 1948, he struck out 25 in a 6–5, 15-inning win against Amsterdam on May 31. He gave up 10 hits, walked 12, and drove in the winning run. The Brooklyn Dodgers drafted him from the Phillies in the 1948 Minor League Draft.

One of my best friends in high school was Billy Fulk, Myerstown, Pennsylvania's best baseball player. Fulk, a catcher, went to West Chester University and attracted baseball scouts, one of which was Lasorda, who was residing in Norristown at the time. On a trip to see the Phillies play, Lasorda invited us to stop by his home. He talked up the Dodgers organization and gave each of us a book, *How To Play The Dodgers Way*. Fulk wound up signing with the Detroit Tigers but never got to the bigs.

Lasorda eventually moved to Los Angeles, and our paths crossed again when he became the Dodgers manager. When in his company, he always made sure to say hello and talk. He often mentioned the visit to his home. He once told me I was the second-best PR person in baseball. "Steve [Brener of the Dodgers] is the best, and you are tied for second with everyone else." Lasorda loved the Dodgers and always preached Dodger blue. One time I reminded him, if he cut his finger, he wouldn't bleed Dodger blue but Phillies red. He didn't like anyone making fun of the Dodgers, and that's why he disliked Phillie Phanatic. People may have felt it was an act when Tommy got angry at the Phanatic. It was no act, folks. Here's what he wrote in his MLB. com blog during the 2005 season: "I hate the Phillie Phanatic. In fact I am not very happy about mascots in general. I think they take away from the game on the field. One of the worst incidents was perpetrated by the Phillie

Phanatic. The Dodgers were in town to play the Phillies, and somehow it got ahold of one of my jerseys. It took the jersey, put it on a dummy, and ran over the dummy again and again. That type of a display should not be shown in ballparks, especially in front of children. It exhibits violence and disrespect. I pulled the Phanatic aside and said, 'Why don't you run over a dummy with a Phillies jersey?' I called the front office of the Phillies and told them how I felt. They can play with kids in the stands, but running over the dummy was simply wrong, and that kids would get the wrong impression. Apparently, they didn't care.

"The next time we were in Philadelphia, I confronted the Phanatic. I told it not to use my jersey anymore, and so the next time he did, I was forced to act. I went right up to it and body slammed it to the turf. I often wondered how it got my jersey and then I found out how. Steve Sax would give it the jerseys because my players thought it was a funny thing to do."

His Phanatic feelings aside, I don't know if I've ever met anyone who was a better ambassador for baseball than Lasorda.

Greg Luzinski

There was a football/baseball player at Notre Dame High School in Niles, Illinois, named Greg Luzinski. He was on the radar for college scholarships and pro baseball teams. Power hitters are hard to come by, and we had him No. 1 on our list of prospects. Owens had seen him play and wanted him badly. In the 1968 draft, we had the 11th selection in the first round. We're in the Commodore Hotel in New York, seated at a round table. Sweating out the first 10 selections was surreal. Our hearts skipped a beat when the New York Mets selected someone from Notre Dame High School with the first pick. Fortunately, it was Notre Dame in Sherman Oaks, California—not Niles— and the player was shortstop Tim Foli.

The Oakland A's, Houston Astros, New York Yankees, Dodgers, Cleveland Indians, Atlanta Braves, and Washington Senators all made their selections, and Luzinski was still on the board. The Baltimore Orioles selected 10th and chose shortstop Junior Kennedy. We could breathe again.

Luzinski was a first baseman then. Owens thought he might move behind the plate but felt we should start him out in pro ball at first base. His first manager was Green in Huron, South Dakota. As it turns out, Green was his last manager, too (in 1980) as we sold Luzinski to the Chicago White Sox before the next season. He had the rare combination of hitting for average and power. Yes, Luzinski struck out; all sluggers do. He was a tremendous clutch hitter. With him and Schmidt in the middle of our lineup, we had a potent one-two power punch for a long time.

Twice he was runner-up to the National League MVP (in 1975 and 1977). He started his postseason career by hitting in 13 consecutive games, still a club record. If Allen was known for his tape-measure home runs at Connie Mack Stadium, Luzinski claimed that honor at the Vet, hitting eight into the upper deck—most of anyone.

Nicknamed the Bull, he purchased over $20,000 in tickets for underprivileged children to see Phillies games in the Bull Ring seats, which were behind him in left field. He was our first winner of the Roberto Clemente Award presented annually by Major League Baseball. Bull is a friendly soul, well-liked by everyone. One of my favorite spring training stories involved him. After a Sunday game in the early 1970s, I returned to the condo on the beach where my family lived. Sitting at the pool with them (a real rarity), I looked toward our first-floor unit, which was left unlocked. Luzinski, who resided in the next building, was walking out of our unit carrying a six-pack of beer under his arm—*our* six-pack from *our* refrigerator! This was how he explained it that day: "My agent was coming for dinner, and I needed some beer." He, though, did pay us back.

His popularity in Philadelphia was folded into our plans for Citizens Bank Park. At Orioles Park in Baltimore, there is a food area in right field called Boog's BBQ manned by their former first baseman, Boog Powell. We decided to emulate that successful eatery with Bull's BBQ located at the east end of Ashburn Alley. He's there every game, greeting fans who are munching on ribs, turkey legs, pulled pork, and his own BBQ sauce and selling Bull's BBQ merchandise. If you go there, don't buy a beer. He'll take it from you.

Roger McDowell

Roger is one of the game's greatest pranksters—probably the best I've seen. He was a master at the hot foot, somehow getting a match in the shoe of his victim, lighting the match, and watching his victim hop and dance. Wheeler once asked McDowell how he did it, but the reliever wouldn't shed any light on his secret.

The best story I have on McDowell came after we signed him to a $1.4 million contract after the 1990 season. We had a press conference at the Vet, and then he and I headed for a banquet appearance in Wilmington, Delaware. While on I-95 near Essington, Pennsylvania, my blue Buick wagon got a flat tire. I pulled off the road and pulled out the spare tire. "Baron, let me do it," McDowell said. Here's our closer, just signed to a new contract, changing a flat tire on I-95 as cars and trucks whizzed by. It was easily the most nerve-wracking tire change of my life. All I needed was for him to get hurt.

Tug McGraw

Frank Edwin McGraw was some kind of a character—and a good relief pitcher, the closer who specialized with a screwball, which sort of fit his personality. I always called him Edwin. He always came right back with "Hey, Leroy." He was a PR person's dream. He had a creative mind and dabbled in various other fields. It seemed as if he was always searching for an identity. On the days that Larry Christenson was starting, he'd walk in the clubhouse and say, "LC, are you pitching today?" LC would respond, "Yes, Tug," setting up McGraw's favorite response, "Well, then so am I."

McGraw also liked to party, but he was there to answer the bell the next day. He came up with names for his pitches. He was the first player to wear green on St. Patrick's Day in spring training. He performed "Casey At Bat" with the Philadelphia Pops orchestra. After his playing career, he was a reporter for Scott Palmer and Channel 6. And he'll forever be remembered for the strikeout that gave the Phillies their first world championship.

And that almost didn't happen. After the 1979 season, Owens and Green felt the club needed a left-handed reliever. "They wanted to trade Tug to the

Texas Rangers for 35-year-old Sparky Lyle," Ruly Carpenter said. "I simply said, 'Sorry boys, but I'm going to step in and say no.'" As it turns out, we acquired Lyle for a player to be named later on September 13, 1980, for the stretch run.

Thirteen years later we'll never forget his emotional final pitch at the closing of Veterans Stadium. Weakened by a brain tumor, McGraw was determined to make one final pitch. Owens died on December 26, 2003, and shortly thereafter McGraw succumbed to cancer. After winning the World Series, Green, Owens, and McGraw were shown on camera crying. Now Owens and McGraw—two men who made their mark at Veterans Stadium—are gone. Neither got to see Citizens Bank Park.

To remember them in our new home, a plaque was placed outside the general manager's box on the press box level in honor of Owens. A bronze plaque was placed on the west wall outside the two bullpens, which is near the steps relievers take to get to the field:

YA GOTTA BELIEVE!
Throughout his challenges
on the mound and in life,
Tug's motto never changed:
"Ya Gotta Believe!"
Mets, 1966–74; Phillies, 1975–84
Frank "Tug" McGraw
August 30, 1944–January 5, 2004

After about five years, the plaque had to be relocated. Light reflected off the plaque, and our bullpen catchers had trouble seeing the ball while warming up relievers. It was then moved into the bench area of our bullpen. Somewhere McGraw was laughing.

Dickie Noles

Selected in the fourth round in 1975 out of a high school in Charlotte, North Carolina, Noles possessed a great arm and was fearless on the mound. In 11 big league seasons, he threw thousands of pitches. But it seems as if he's remembered for one, a pitch that came on a big stage.

In Game 4 of the 1980 World Series in Kansas City, a game the Royals won to even the series at 2–2, Noles replaced Christenson in the first inning during a four-run outburst. In the second inning, Noles gave up a solo home run to Willie Aikens, his second in two innings. It was the lone run off Noles in more than four innings. In the fourth inning, Noles got two quick strikes on George Brett and then brushed back the KC superstar, knocking him on his butt. Noles sent a message. After that pitch the Royals scored in only three of the next 23 innings before losing the series at the Vet.

Years later Noles, Pete Rose, and Brett were scheduled to sign autographs at the Phillies Phestival, the annual charity event that raises funds to strike out ALS. "We were in the visiting clubhouse at the Vet," Noles said. "I hadn't seen or talked with George and was nervous about meeting him. Pete saw George walk into the room, 'Hey, Dickie, there's the guy you knocked on his ass.' George had his back to me. When he turned around, he had glued a plastic baseball on his right cheek. It certainly broke the ice."

When the Royals opened the Phillies 2013 season at Citizens Bank Park, Brett and Schmidt were brought in to throw out the ceremonial first pitch. Noles delivered the ball to Brett. The night before, the three were out to dinner with some of the Phillies ownership group. "With Mike Schmidt and George Brett, two Hall of Fame third basemen, I figured I should be a spectator and not one to talk a lot," Noles said. "During dinner George came over to me, knelt on one knee, and said, 'Did you really throw at me?' I said, 'Yes.' He came right back, 'I loved it,' and then gave me a big hug [and said] 'What people don't remember is that you struck me out on the next pitch, a nasty slider.' I tell you what. You can't find a nicer person than George Brett."

Noles experienced a lot of ups and downs in his personal life, but to his credit turned his life around to become a valuable employee working with our minor league players. He's a nationally recognized motivational speaker who often talks about the dangers of substance abuse. He donates a lot of his time to helping kids.

Pete Rose

Pete Rose was with the Phillies for five seasons, which were five enjoyable seasons for me. His middle name is Edward, and that's what I used to call him. He was extremely cooperative with the media and always at his locker after a game—whether we won or lost, or he had two hits, or went hitless.

I don't believe I ever saw a hitter with better concentration and drive. If he got hits in his first two at-bats, that wasn't enough. If he got three and it was a lopsided game, he bore down to get four. After we signed him following the 1978 season, media flocked to Clearwater for the next spring training. We were a good team that now added a great player. The first time the Cincinnati Reds came to Jack Russell Memorial Stadium, we had so many fans that we roped off an area behind the left fielder to allow for standing room. Any ball hit into the crowd or that rolled into the crowd was a ground-rule double.

At spring training our son, Andy, was the bat boy for a couple of games. Rose came up to Andy in the dugout one game. "Hey, kid, between innings, get me a hot dog," he said in handing Andy a $5 bill. When Andy handed him the hot dog during the next half-inning, Pete said, "Keep the change."

With the team in New York to play the Mets in 1979, Rose's agent, Reuven Katz, called me in Philadelphia. "I need to talk to Pete. [His wife] Carolyn is filing for a divorce," Katz said. "He doesn't answer his hotel phone." Remember, there were no cell phones back then. So I called Wheeler, who was with the team. "All kinds of people had been trying to reach Pete all day to tell him his wife had filed divorce papers," Wheeler said, retelling the story. "You asked me to go to his room and give it a shot. I knocked on his door several times. Finally I heard that familiar voice in a very low tone say, 'Yeah, who is it?' I said, 'It's Wheels. I have to tell you something.' The door opened slightly, held by the chain. I saw those unmistakable eyes look out, and he said, 'What's up Wheels?' I told him what had happened. He said, 'Okay, thanks. See you on the bus.'"

Did the divorce affect Rose? Well, he went 3-for-4, 2-for-3, and 4-for-5 in the three-game series. He finished 1979, hitting in 26 of his last 27 games and was named the National League Player of the Month when he hit .421 and recorded an astounding 51 hits. Earlier that same season, I was in Ozark's office before a game. Schmidt couldn't play that night, and Ozark asked Rose to play third. Rose came in the office smiling, "Danny, you know third base is a long way from first base. I hope I can get there." Despite that funny line, Rose knew everything about the next game: who was pitching, what he threw, pitch sequences and who was hot, cold, or injured. His response was simple, "Why shouldn't I? Baseball's my business."

On August 10, 1981, baseball resumed after a lengthy strike. Rose knew he needed one more hit to break Stan Musial's National League record. The long 55-game strike was about to end with a bang. Veterans Stadium was packed as was the press box for an ABC game against St. Louis to start the second half of the season. Rose hit a single between shortstop and third base in the eighth inning off Mark Littell for his 3,631st hit, surpassing Musial, who set the record in a Cardinals uniform.

The game was halted as Rose was acknowledged by the throng of 60,561. Musial was escorted to first base where he congratulated the Phillies first baseman. Pete Rose Jr. came out of the dugout to hug his dad, and fireworks filled the sky. "The fireworks went off in the first inning," Rose said. "The scoreboard thought it was a hit, but it was ruled an error. The whole thing about breaking records is the reaction of the fans. It was very special because it happened at home in front of so many Phillies fans. Musial being there was icing on the cake. There was no pressure attached to this record. It's not like a hitting streak. I needed one more hit, and it was going to happen. It was just a matter of where, when, the kind of hit, and the pitcher."

Following the game, we had an interview room set up in a large room behind home plate to accommodate the media mass. He looked at me as we walked toward the room and asked, "You got the President calling?" I responded, "I don't know." But Rose really did know everything. Ronald Reagan was supposed to call on a phone we had next to the podium, but the White House said it was subject to last-minute changes. Shortly after the start of the press conference, the special red phone rang. It was the White House. A historic moment turned into a hilarious one.

White House operator: Mr. Rose, hold on please…
Rose: Tell the president, I'll be with him in a minute.

Pete Rose awaits a phone call from President Reagan during a postgame press conference in 1981 after Rose broke Stan Musial's National League record for career hits. It was the most entertaining press conference I've ever seen.

White House: Mr. Rose, hold on please…

Rose: Good thing there isn't a missile on the way.

White House: Mr. Rose, hold on please…

Rose: I've waited 19 years for this. I can wait another minute.

White House: Mr. Rose, hold on please…

Rose: Larry, I'll give him my home phone.

White House: Hello Pete, this is President Reagan calling.

Rose: Hey, how ya' doing? (That response brought down the house.)

Interestingly, Musial's 3,630th hit came on September 29, 1963, the Cardinals' final game of the season and his last game. It was a sixth-inning, ground ball single to right past a rookie second baseman on the Reds named Pete Rose.

Leading up to Rose's record-setting night, a restaurant owner from South Jersey called. He had read that Musial was in town dining on lobster at

Bookbinder's Restaurant. He wanted to present Rose with a lobster after he broke the record. I agreed but told him it might be an hour or more because of the press conference. He was fine with that. Once the press conference was over and we were back in the clubhouse, I introduced the restaurant owner, who brought an 18-pound lobster—one pound for each of Pete's years in the majors—into the clubhouse. It was the biggest thing I ever saw. Rose took one look and asked, "That thing isn't going to take a shit in my Rolls, will it?" Only Rose could come up with a comment like that.

Rose tied Musial's record on June 10 (the last day before the strike) at the Vet with a first-inning single off Ryan. The pitcher, now enshrined in the Hall of Fame, looked at Rose on first base and touched the bill of his hat, essentially saying, "Nice going, but that's it." Ryan struck out Rose each of the next three at-bats with a mixture of blazing fastballs and back-breaking curveballs. I was in the dugout behind where Green was standing in case Rose broke the record. I had never been in the dugout before during the game. I was blown away by Ryan's performance.

On one Saturday I received a call from the Milton Hershey Medical Center. A young boy who worshiped Rose was seriously ill and was in the hospital. There was a request: "Is there any chance Pete could speak with the boy on the phone?" Rose said no problem. We went into the manager's office and made the call. Driving in for a Sunday afternoon game the next day, KYW Radio reported the young boy had died. I went to the clubhouse to let Rose know, but he already heard it on KYW Radio.

His career had Hall of Fame written all over it. After all, he is the hit king. Banned from baseball for allegedly betting on baseball games as a manager, Cooperstown can't display his plaque. Betting on baseball is against the rules. Those rules are posted in every clubhouse every year, and Major League Baseball verbally reviews the rules every spring training in front of every player. Yes, Pete was wrong. But if a player who used performance-enhancing drugs gets into Cooperstown, why shouldn't Peter Edward? He had 4,256 hits and 0 PEDs.

Juan Samuel

What an exciting player. I can still see him flying around the bases, legging out a triple or stealing a base. He was electrifying. His personality never changed, always up and always smiling. He would call me "Schwenk" and follow that with a big smile. To everyone he is "Sammy." It broke me up when his son was born. He named him Samuel Samuel.

His personality, though, did change when we made him a center fielder. Yes, he wasn't a Manny Trillo on defense at second base, but no one matched his offense until a guy named Chase Utley came along. The transition took place in spring training. Playing the outfield in Florida can be tricky. High skies can be blinding, and there were windy conditions in the open ballparks as opposed to the larger, closed ballparks in the major leagues. Veteran outfielders have been known to struggle on those types of days. Samuel was going to play center field on a sunny, windy day at Jack Russell Stadium. He walked out of the clubhouse, looked at the sky, and then said to me, "Here, you take de glove." Then he flashed the infectious smile.

Not being able to speak Spanish is one of my weaknesses. Wheeler can speak the language and he can communicate with the Latin players in their tongue. To me that shows you respect them. Oh, well, next time around, I'll learn Spanish. Samuel tried to teach me one time, but I failed. He was a good teacher; I was a poor student. Samuel has a special place in my heart. When my mother died in 2004, he sent flowers to the funeral service. He was coaching with the Detroit Tigers at the time. That's a true and classy friend.

John Vukovich

I thought Vukovich's fielding at third base in 1980 was his best tool. As the season unfolded, though, I realized his best asset. He was a tough son-of-a-gun who wasn't afraid to get on teammates. Green wanted him on the team "to help carry my message." When Green went to the Cubs, so did Vukovich. He was inches away from being the Cubs manager when Green quit over a dispute with the Tribune Company, which owned the Cubs. But Vukovich returned home in 1988 and started the longest tenure as a coach in our history.

Vukovich was the most beloved and respected person ever to wear our uniform. He knew how to play the game and was a great teacher. He could pat players on their back but also get on their butt. He became a brother to me, always available to talk. Once in a while, he'd stop by the office before going to the clubhouse. "I haven't seen you for a couple days," he asked once. "Are you alright?" I vividly recall another visit. "You're down. I can tell," I said. "Do you want to talk about it?...Come on, let's talk." He closed the door, and we chatted. As tough as he could be at times, he was a man with a big heart and a sense of humor. The only thing he loved more than the Phillies was his family. He coached for countless managers and was loyal to everyone, never once hoping he would get a chance to replace his friend when a change was made.

His wife, Bonnie, was an usherette at the Vet when they met. She wasn't a student of the game initially. One time she was in the stands with Vukovich's brother. Vukovich came to bat and hit a high pop-up in the field. Bonnie stood up and cheered. His brother cautioned Bonnie it was an out. "Yes," she replied. "But he hit it so high." Please understand, Bonnie: we are laughing with you and not at you. But I'm sure Vukovich schooled her during their time together.

Whenever assignments were made for the ALS autograph party, I always put Vukovich with Lenny Dykstra, knowing Dykstra would want to bolt before the two-hour autograph time had elapsed. Like clockwork, Vukovich would seek me out and ask, "Why me? I thought I was your friend?" Vukovich was an awesome storyteller. He was a coach with the Cubs when Don Zimmer was the manager. On a flight to San Francisco, Zimmer had a little too much to drink. "We're on the same floor in the hotel, a couple doors away from each other," Vukovich said. "Zimmer goes to the wrong door. When he inserts his key, the red light comes on. He said, 'Damn it. I'm not even in the room and I already have a phone message.'" Vukovich always followed that story with a deep laugh.

Vukovich's life ended way too short. He was a competitor as a player and he battled brain cancer as long as he could. He died on March 8, 2007. We were in spring training. The Phillies are a very caring family. We chartered a plane to take many of us in Clearwater to New Jersey for the funeral, and anyone from another club training on Florida's West Coast was welcome on the charter.

Bobby Wine

I don't think I ever saw a shortstop with a better arm than Bobby Wine. It was a rifle. Offensively, he struggled. Getting beaned in the minors didn't help. He played his entire career in the majors under Mauch, first with us and then with the Montreal Expos. "Gene taught me everything I know about baseball," Wine said. "He expected everyone to be like him, thinking baseball 24 hours a day." After his playing career, "Wine-o" coached for us, serving as the bench coach for Green and Owens. He never got a shot at managing in the majors, which I don't understand; neither does he.

We became friends as did our wives. Some people think Fran and Julie look like sisters; that's not true. I'm six days older than Bobby. Some people think I look younger; that's true. Fran and Bobby rented Lasorda's house in Norristown for a few years and later bought it. We had many cookouts and parties there. In spring training they always rented a house on Clearwater beach, and we had fun times then, too. Fun could be Bobby's middle name. He loved being a prankster and loved to tell stories.

Back in 1964 Sandy Koufax was throwing a no-hitter at us at Connie Mack Stadium. Tony Taylor led off the ninth by striking out. Ruben Amaro was out on a foul pop-up to first. Mauch needed a pinch-hitter. "Gene came down the dugout and said, 'Grab a bat. You're gonna hit.' I was hitting around .200, and he's sending me to try and break up a no-hitter? I fouled off the first pitch, and it hit Eddie Vargo, the home-plate umpire, in the neck. He went down to one knee, Joe [Liscio, the Phillies trainer] came out. Eddie said, 'I'm okay. Let's go, don't want [Koufax] to get cold.' I guess he didn't care about me. The next two pitches, I never saw," Wine said.

After Mauch left managing, he ran into Wine. "Was I really as bad as people say?" Mauch asked. Wine had a great retort. "If you have a couple of hours, I can tell you." That wasn't the only amusing interaction between Wine and Mauch. "Turk [reliever Dick Farrell] lived in Houston. We had a day off before flying to Houston," Wine said. "In those days we flew on the day of the game, many times on a commercial flight. Turk asked Gene if he could fly ahead of the team to spend a day at his home with his family. Gene said, 'Sure.' Turk didn't stop but should have. [He said:] 'Can Gene Oliver go with

25

me? He's gonna mow my lawn.' Mauch didn't hesitate: 'You may go—no for Oliver.'"

One of my favorite Wine stories is from the bus ride. "We're in Houston at the Astrodome. Dallas [Green] was our player rep, and [with] any gripes, we went to him," Wine said. "We were never sure when the bus would leave after a game. Sometimes it was 30 minutes or 45 or an hour or more. Dallas called a meeting of players and coaches. Mauch wasn't included. We all agreed that the bus would always leave one hour after the game. That way everybody knew. [The] game ended, and Dallas let everyone know: '10:50 bus.' We showered, dressed, and headed for the bus. It's now 11 o'clock, and we're sitting in the bus. No one else is coming, and Gene isn't there. So we complained to Dallas, who finally said, 'Okay, bussie, let's go.' The driver got lost, trying to get out of the Astrodome parking lot. He wound up circling back to where we started. There was Gene, standing by himself, smoking a cigarette. The driver opened the door, and Gene climbed in. He gave all of us a lecture: 'From now on, the bus will leave when I tell it to and not before!' I looked back at Dallas, and he just threw his hands in the air."

During spring training Julie and I invited Fran and Bobby and Ginny and Danny Ozark for dinner. As they are about to enter our beach house, Danny asked Bobby, "What's Baron's wife's name?" Bobby responded, "Karen." In walked Danny. "Karen, good to see you again," he said. All night long Julie was Karen.

When Wine was a coach, Wheeler was one of his favorite targets. As soon as Wheeler set his typewriter or briefcase on the ground while in the airport or waiting for a bus, Wine would sneak up and take it. Wheeler would panic, but no one would rat on Wine. Eventually, everything was returned to him. "For some reason we liked to pick on Wheels," Wine said. "But once on the flight, we'd sit next to each other and talk about the game."

Wine also coached under Green when he managed the Mets. He then went to work for the Braves and spent 14 seasons as their advance scout working with Bobby Cox. No one knew the National League better than Wine. He retired in 2011 to his Norristown home to spend time with his first love—his wife, children, grandchildren, and great-grandchildren.

CHAPTER 2
COOPERSTOWN PARADE

Between 1976 and 1983, the Phillies had a run of six postseason appearances. We also had a similar run in the village of Cooperstown, New York, home of the National Baseball Hall of Fame and Museum. Steve Carlton (1994), Richie Ashburn (1995), Mike Schmidt (1995), and Jim Bunning (1996) were enshrined in Cooperstown in that decade, making it the greatest Hall of Fame decade in our history. During the next decade, Harry Kalas received the prestigious Ford C. Frick Award for broadcasting excellence (2002). Then general manager Pat Gillick was inducted into the Hall of Fame (2011). Robin Roberts was inducted in 1976.

I made a trip to Cooperstown early in the 1994 season to learn the ropes. My role was to arrange housing accommodations, credentials, and seating for Phillies executives, employees, and my family. In 1995 I had to get Roberts, Ashburn, Schmidt, and Carlton together for a photo on the lawn of the Otesaga Hotel. That photo is on display in the Cooperstown Gallery of the Hall of Fame Club in Citizens Bank Park.

The museum is filled with artifacts and history. One display includes World Series rings down through the years. My wife and I were privileged to deliver our 2008 World Series ring to the museum early in the 2009 season. There was a small bunch of Phillies fans there that day, and they just couldn't get enough photos of the ring.

Robin Roberts (inducted in 1976)

Robin Evan Roberts did things that a Phillies pitcher will never duplicate. Starting in 1950 he won 20 or more games six consecutive seasons. In each of those seasons, he threw 300 or more innings. He was the Opening Day starting pitcher 12 straight years. On September 6, 1952, the Phillies beat the Boston Braves 7–6 in 17 innings. He pitched all 17 innings. That game was part of a streak of 28 consecutive complete games over two seasons. Between starts he threw batting practice.

Roberts simply took the ball every four days and delivered. No. 36 was so reliable. One of his best friends on the Whiz Kids, coach Maje McDonnell, loved to talk about him. "On the mound, he'd fight 'til the end of the earth. Off the field you couldn't believe [it]—perfect gentleman," McDonnell said. "[He] went to hospitals on his own without people asking. He would gladly visit a children's ward. He just didn't want publicity. But, boy, did he hate to lose. There were many times after a loss, Robbie would come up to me, 'Maje, let's go.' We'd walk back to the hotel no matter how far the hotel was from the ballpark. Sometimes, we'd walk the streets until six in the morning and then get breakfast. Once in a while, he would mutter, 'Why did I throw him that pitch?'"

Others have said he was also stubborn on the mound. He wouldn't back hitters off the plate, simply challenged them all the time. He gave up 505 home runs, a major league mark that stood until Jamie Moyer broke it in 2010. Roberts also had a sense of humor. It was evident in part of his Hall of Fame acceptance speech in 1976: "The Hall of Fame people, I'd like to say, were very nice," Roberts said. "I only had one request that they turned down: I asked if it would be appropriate if I would invite everyone that ever hit a home run off me to be here today, but Cooperstown wasn't big enough. But I am going to have little cards made up that say 'I hit a home run off Robbie' and mail them to all those gentlemen because I'm sure they'd like to have it in their wallet. There were a lot of them, by the way."

For some reason, none of us in the front office went to Cooperstown when he was inducted. He never said anything about it. When he had an opinion, however, he wouldn't hold back. I had been around Roberts numerous times but really didn't get to know him well until we began the alumni weekend tradition. He was the most unassuming Hall of Famer you could meet. He just was a very nice person through and through. He never wanted to be treated like a prima donna. He was a humble legend, who smiled easily and laughed a lot.

We talked about getting him more involved with the Phillies again. We came up with a plan where he would come to Philadelphia for four days during alumni weekend and two other days during a season. He'd be willing to play golf or have a meal with our sponsors or clients. "You don't know how pleased I am working for the Phillies again," he said. "If you need me anytime, just let me know. I'll be up [from my Tampa, Florida, home] from time to time." During All-Star Games the Phillies often took clients to the games.

Roberts always went to those games and was more than willing to spend time with that group.

We had a lot of conversations during spring training, alumni weekends, Hall of Fame weekends, and over the phone. His recall of pitches and plays from his career was unmatched. I loved to listen to his stories. I learned that when he was sold to the New York Yankees in spring training of 1961 owner Bob Carpenter said no one would ever wear No. 36 again. Since there were no official ceremonies, we saluted Roberts during alumni night in 2008 and officially retired the number. That number, by the way, is also retired at Michigan State University and from the Wilmington Blue Rocks, his first pro team in 1948.

We talked about his 17-inning complete game, in which he gave up 18 hits and six runs while walking three and striking out five. "We won the game when Del Ennis hit a home run into the upper deck off Bob Chipman. We didn't count pitches back then, so I don't know how many I threw. I do know I pitched better in the second game [during the last eight innings] than I did in the first game," he said, chuckling. "I always took a hot shower and ran hot water on my arm. I was told one time that it would increase circulation. I did the same thing my whole career. It's hard to say that was right, and the ice they use today is wrong."

Roberts loved the 2008–2009 Phillies. He didn't miss a game on television. He'd often call the next morning, "Jimmy can really play shortstop, can't he?" Roberts said. "I love the way Chase plays"…"Ryan is some kind of strong. Did you see where that ball landed?"…"Shane can fly, can't he?"…"I wish I had Brad's slider"…"My man Jayson is some kind of athlete." My favorite was: "If I had Cole's change, I'd still be pitching."

He called Jayson Werth "my man" because they were from the same hometown, Springfield, Illinois. Roberts knew some of Werth's relatives, and they often chatted when Roberts was around the ballclub. We brought Roberts, Schmidt, Carlton, and Bunning—our living Hall of Famers—to Citizens Bank Park for the World Series in both 2008 and 2009. For my Phillies Insider blog, I thought it would be a good idea to have Roberts comment after each 2008 game. Since he lived in Tampa, he knew a lot about the Rays.

When I approached him, he quickly replied, "Sure." He'd email his comments after each game in time for me to post the blog early the following morning.

When we won it all in 2008, the organization decided to give the four Hall of Famers World Series rings. They were so very appreciative, especially Roberts and Bunning, who never were on a world championship club. When we played the Yankees in the 2009 series, we included Roberts as part of the traveling party to New York. He was a link to the 1950 Phillies-Yankees World Series. The *TODAY Show* was interested in having him on the air live before one of the games in New York. We got up early, took a limo to the studio where he appeared with Tino Martinez, the former Yankees player. It turned out that Martinez lived in Tampa, too, and they knew each other. During bus rides, hotel stays, late nights, and long walks at Yankee Stadium to our seats in a suite, I noticed Roberts was slowing a bit. I suggested a wheelchair to ease his walk at the stadium, but he refused. Was it stubbornness or pride? Probably both.

After that 2008 year, we traded for Roy Halladay. Roberts often drove from Tampa to Clearwater, Florida, to see spring training games at Bright House Field. "Baron, I'm coming tomorrow," Roberts said. "I would like to meet Halladay and talk pitching. What time should I be there?" He loved to hang around the team and chat with the players. "Every time he came around the clubhouse he would start talking about pitching," Brad Lidge said. "He talked with me about my slider, and anything he had to say, I was all ears. Another thing about Robbie was that he never talked about the way things were when he played the game. He realized that the game changed with time. I was really fortunate to be able to talk with a living legend about pitching."

During spring training in 2010, I called Roberts and said I'd like to have dinner near his Tampa home to chat some more about our alumni programs. Baseball 101 For Women is a highly successful program the Phillies had been holding twice a season at Citizens Bank Park. My idea was to launch an alumni luncheon for seniors. Roberts was all ears and eager to participate in our first such luncheon during that season. I don't recall the specific date other than it was late in the 2010 Grapefruit League schedule when he came to see the game. I asked if he would sign three dozen baseballs that we could use for special occasions. He gladly signed. That game was the last he saw in person, and the baseballs were the last he signed for us before died on May 6. He never got to be part of our first alumni luncheon. I had lost a great friend and wouldn't be getting any more phone calls. It was an empty feeling.

A memorial service was held near his Tampa home. Several of us from the front office wanted to be there to pay our last respects to a great Phillie and a dear friend. Pastor Wally Meyer pointed to the right side of the sanctuary, "Robbie would sit in the last row every week, providing he arrived early enough," Meyer said. "We all know he had 305 complete games. I once told him I had more complete services than 305. He laughed and said, 'Yes, but you didn't have umpires.' Yes, he pitched a lot of complete games. He also led a complete life."

The youngest of Robbie's four sons is Jim. He spoke last and made a touching comment: "Mom died five years ago next month right around Father's Day," he said. "Dad died near Mother's Day. He just decided he was going back with her."

Steve Carlton (1994)

GM John Quinn, director of minor leagues and scouting Paul Owens, and their wives were dining at the Garden Seat restaurant in Clearwater prior to the start of spring training in 1972. The Phillies were having a tough time signing right-handed pitcher Rick Wise, and the St. Louis Cardinals called to see if the Phillies would be interested in trading Wise for Steve Carlton, who was also in a contract squabble. During dinner that night, Quinn relayed the Cardinals conversation to Owens. "Would you trade Wise for Carlton?" Quinn asked. Owens quickly responded, "What are you waiting for?"

The trade wasn't very popular. "Lefty" got off to a 5–1 start but lost five in a row as the offense scored 10 total runs. Then he turned in the most impressive one-season pitching performance in Phillies history, winning 15 straight games at one point. He finished with 27 wins out of our 59. He was "Super Steve" on a very mediocre team. When Carlton was pitching, Larry Bowa used to say it was "Win-day."

After that season the Phillies signed Carlton to a $165,000 contract, the most money ever for a pitcher. How times have changed. Carlton was the most cooperative player I'd been around that incredible year. He did endless interviews and appearances during the season and that winter. After getting burned by the media a few years later, he decided not to talk anymore. I remember him saying, "I give my time, and they take my words out of context. Why should I continue to take time for them? Without quotes they can be more creative in their writing." He not only took their slams personally, but he also thought he concentrated better without the distraction of speaking to reporters.

He opted to not talk and stuck to it, and his stance actually made my life easier. "Policy is policy" was his motto. Knowing he was an avid hunter, *Sports Illustrated* wanted to do a story about him hunting. "Policy is policy" was our response. *SI* tried again to appeal to his wine aficionado tastes, thinking a story focusing on his love of wine would get him to talk, but he declined again. Ralph Bernstein was a hard-hitting Associated Press sportswriter in Philadelphia. For many spring trainings, he would approach Carlton, "Steve, look, no notebook, no pen, no tape recorder. Can we talk?" Carlton would put his left hand on Ralph's right shoulder and say, "Ralph, policy is policy." Because he was consistent with his stance, the media accepted and respected him.

Carlton was the most focused athlete I've seen. On the mound he was oblivious to everything. At one point he put in ear plugs to block out the crowd's noise. He worked fast, something he had learned from Bob Gibson with the Cardinals. He needed three strikeouts to reach 3,000 and become the sixth pitcher ever to reach that lofty height. All the others were right-handers. His first pitch came at 7:40 PM against the Montreal Expos on April 29, 1981. Always a fast worker, Carlton left little doubt as he struck out the side on 16 pitches in four minutes. Tim Raines went down swinging, Jerry Manuel was called out, and Tim Wallach took a 3–2 pitch for strike three.

The crowd rose to its feet, the scoreboard flashed a message about 3,000 strikeouts, and Carlton stepped back off the mound and tipped his cap to the appreciative fans. He came back in the dugout after that inning. Manager Dallas Green said, "Now that it's over, let's win the game." He did. When he overtook Nolan Ryan for the most strikeouts on June 7, 1983, the information was immediately displayed on Phanavision. Fans gave him a standing ovation, and Carlton stepped off the mound again and tipped his cap. After the game he asked, "Now what did I do?" Individual records were immaterial. Winning was his ultimate goal.

He had a deadly slider. When asked how he delivered it, he'd simply say, "I grab the ball like this and then throw the crap out of it." Willie Stargell once said trying to hit that slider was like eating soup with a fork."

In 1983 he was closing in on 300 wins. I approached him in the clubhouse when he was at 299. I asked, "Lefty, what are we going to do after you win your 300th?" "Go for 400," he responded. "Lefty, I know that, but that's not what I mean. What about talking to the media?" He paused, "Talking to the fans would be more appealing," he said. My wheels were spinning. "Okay," I said, "How about this scenario? After the game, Harry Kalas [who Carlton loved] will interview you. I'll take questions from the media, give them to Harry. You answer, and the fans learn." Another pause before Carlton finally said, "Okay."

His 300th was going to come on the road, which was good news. The media circus would be smaller. I decided to let the media know the postgame plan in advance. The next day *The Philadelphia Inquirer* had a five-column headline, "Lefty To Talk After 300th Win." A suburban paper wrote that the interview resembled a "Communistic-controlled news conference." That afternoon a call came from the clubhouse: "Lefty wants to see you." Lefty was in the weight room where he did his daily rigorous workouts. "Did you see the paper? They are making a big deal out of me speaking. We're trying to win a pennant. That's more important than an individual record. Let's forget it." Carlton's eyes can light up with his laugh. They can also be piercing, providing an answer without saying a word. I got the message from those eyes. Carlton is a very unique individual, a deep thinker with some strange theories at times. But one thing was consistent with him: you laughed when you were around him.

He put up Hall of Fame numbers. When he was finished playing, he was a first-ballot inductee in 1994. As was customary the new inductees were expected to attend a press conference in New York the day after the announcement. Carlton asked me to be there and also in Cooperstown. I guess I was his security blanket. We had dinner in his suite the night before. He seemed very excited. I attempted to coach him on some of the potential questions he would face, especially why is he talking now after not doing so most of his career. His focus wasn't there, so there was no use in pushing my case. The next day he stood behind the microphone and answered question after question. After 30 minutes the president of the Baseball Writers Association of America asked me to end the press conference. I stepped forward and announced we had time for one more question. He gently pushed me aside, "No, let's keep going." He did. I'm not sure why he was so accommodating to the media other than the fact he was clearly enjoying himself.

When he got to the podium on induction day, Carlton began by saying, "This is a very special moment for me. Most of you probably don't know that I got my big break in baseball right here in Cooperstown. Back in the spring of 1966, I had been sent down by the Cardinals to work on a few things in the minor leagues. It just so happened that the Cardinals played in an exhibition game here that year against the Twins, and the Cardinals invited me up from Tulsa to pitch in that game. I had the good fortune to strike out 10 Twins in seven innings that precipitated my return to the major leagues…Memory is baseball's fourth dimension, and I know the memory of this day will be with my family and me forever. Thank you so much. You are very kind."

Mike Schmidt (1995)

Michael Jack Schmidt's road from Dayton, Ohio, to Philadelphia wasn't a smooth one. First as a six-year-old, he fell out of a tree. While slipping he grabbed onto uninsulated wires, carrying 4,000 volts. Fortunately, he was wearing sneakers. The juice went right through him into the ground. Aside from some burn scars, he survived and was back in school the next day.

Twice in football, as a sophomore and the following year, he sustained injured knees. He hurt the right one first. Then he was off to Ohio University with two bad knees to study architecture and possibly play basketball. During his freshman year, an athletic trainer, doctor, and insurance man told Schmidt he'd have to leave the team because he was too much of a risk physically.

Told to strengthen each knee, Schmidt began physical therapy and two months later he was a switch-hitting shortstop on the baseball team. Starting during Schmidt's high school career, the late Tony Lucadello, our scout in the Midwest, began following Schmidt. He knew he was a good athlete. Lucadello once reported, "Mike played hard and didn't like to lose. He had trouble hitting off-speed and breaking stuff, but he'd battle you. He was always out there before the game, working hard. He loved the game."

As the 1971 summer draft approached, Owens, then the director of minor leagues and scouting, went to see Schmidt play. Lucadello had Schmidt rated as his No. 1 prospect, and Owens wanted to see for himself. "He hit a home run and two or three other hits in a doubleheader," Owens reported. "He was a shortstop, but to me he was going to make an ideal third baseman." On Owens list of the top prospects, he moved Schmidt to No. 2 behind a 6'5" right-hander from California, Roy Thomas.

The Phillies had the sixth overall selection in the first round and chose Thomas. He signed with the Phillies but never pitched for them. When Owens, however, became general manager, he put him in a package to acquire veteran lefty Jim Kaat in 1975. In the second round of the 1971 draft, the Phillies had the 30th pick. The Chicago White Sox had the 25th to start the round. Owens held his breath. The Kansas City Royals were 29th and when their turn came they grabbed a third baseman who would become a Hall of Famer, George Brett. With the 30th pick, Owens was glad to announce Schmidt's name.

Schmidt played in Double A ball at Reading, Pennsylvania, that summer and hit a home run against the Phillies in an exhibition game. He spent most of 1972 in Triple A but was called up in September. Schmidt never saw the minor leagues again, though many thought he belonged there when he batted .196 during his rookie season in 1973. A kid from Dayton survived two bad knees but had some rough times in Philadelphia, getting booed by fans and hassled by the media. He once said, "Only in Philadelphia can you experience the thrill of victory and the agony of reading about it the next day." Considered cool and a little aloof, fans rarely saw the other side of a talented athlete.

Schmidt faced considerable media attention because of his status as a superstar. One writer working on a book about hitting was coming to Florida in spring training to interview Ted Williams, Al Kaline, and Stan Musial and was interested in talking with Schmidt. It seemed legitimate enough. When I mentioned it to Schmidt, he said, "You make it easy for the media to get to a superstar." He said it with a smile on his face, which I took to mean he was half serious, half kidding.

Schmidt wound up as the greatest player in Phillies history and a Hall of Famer on the first ballot. His name dominates the Phillies record book, including wearing the pinstriped uniform for 18 seasons. No one else has matched that. It would stand to reason that if Schmitty had the most home runs in our history (548), he would have the most walk-off homers. Two of his 10 walk-offs were certainly special. On Opening Day in 1974, he unloaded a two-run, game-winner off the New York Mets' Tug McGraw, who, of course, would later star for us, to win the game 5–4. Nine years later he had a most unusual game-winner, another two-run job. Hitless in his last 22 at-bats, Schmidt struck out the first four times on 12 pitches before hitting the 13th pitch for a dramatic two-run homer off the Expos' Jeff Reardon and the 5–3 win.

When Schmidt made his debut in 1972, he wore No. 22. He changed to No. 20 the following season. When he hit the game-winner off McGraw, he was batting eighth. With deceptive speed he also was the leadoff hitter one time and once stole three bases in a game. Oddly, his first home run and last one came at Veterans Stadium, but all the milestone ones—No. 100, 200, 300, 400, and 500—occurred on the road. His first and 500th home runs came with runners on base. The other milestone ones were solo shots.

He came through big time in the 1980 pennant race during a three-game, season-ending, decisive series in Montreal. On a Friday night he homered and drove in a run with a sacrifice fly as we won 2–1. After a long, long rain delay during the next afternoon, we clinched another National League East title because Schmidt blasted a two-run homer for the game-winner.

Gene Mauch once said exceptional athletes do exceptional things. Michael Jack certainly fit that. As his career marched on, the home run numbers kept climbing. Vince Nauss, a member of the public relations department, was on the road for Schmidt's big ones. No. 400 came in Los Angeles off Dodgers right-hander Bob Welch. The ball landed in the seats but bounced back on the field. Dodgers center fielder Ken Landreaux threw the ball back in the stands.

Wanting to get the ball for Schmidt, Nauss spoke with the Dodgers security staff and was able to retrieve the historic ball.

Schmidt couldn't have written a more dramatic script for his 500th home run. When he faced Don Robinson of the Pittsburgh Pirates in Three Rivers Stadium, the Phillies were trailing 6–5 on April 18, 1987. Two runners were on base with two out in the top of the ninth when Schmidt stepped into the batter's box. He drilled a 3–0 pitch for a game-winning home run. I can still hear Kalas' call: "There it is—the career 500th home run for Michael Jack Schmidt."

Knowing No. 500 was coming, we had Jerry Clothier, vice president, finance, get a $500 bill from the federal reserve. Nauss put it in his wallet and slept with the wallet. The bill was to be presented to the fan that caught the ball along with a personally autographed bat from Schmidt during a postgame press conference. Well, the historic ball landed in our bullpen, and pitcher Joe Cowley retrieved it. "Unfortunately, I had to tell Joe, 'Club personnel didn't qualify for the $500 bill,'" Nauss said, laughing.

Two years later Nauss was on the road again with the team. He called me on Memorial Day from San Diego, "Baron, you'll never guess what's about to happen." I thought we might have made a big trade. "No," Nauss said. "Schmitty is retiring." Schmidt met with the media in San Diego and then flew home for a press conference with the Philadelphia media the next day. I decided we needed to do something special. A press conference in a room at the Vet didn't fit. So we put a podium at home plate where he made his mark. Instead of facing the pitcher, he faced the stands and the media that packed the warning track. As Schmidt came up to the podium, I whispered, "There's a box of tissue under the podium if you need it." He did.

His career was over, and many of us shed a tear. More tears flowed when he and Ashburn were inducted into the Baseball Hall of Fame. Cooperstown became a sea of red as Phillies fans poured out in record numbers that weekend. During Schmidt's speech he touched on a lot of topics, including Phillies Nation. "What about the Phillies fans? I know you're out there," he said. "I've seen your caps, your license plates, your cars, your smiling faces for the past three days. You have stretched the city limits of Philadelphia all the way to

Cooperstown. It's unbelievable. I'm asked about you fans, about what it was like to play in Philadelphia. If I had it do all over again, I would do it in Philly. If I had to do it all over again, the only thing I would change would be me. I'd be less sensitive, more outgoing. I'd be more appreciative of what you expected from me. My relationship with Philadelphia fans has always been misunderstood. Can we put that to rest here today? I sure hope we can."

Richie Ashburn (1995)

Ashburn is a Phillies icon. When you think about it, Ashburn touched more lives in the Delaware Valley than anyone else in sports. As a baseball player, broadcaster, and sports columnist for the *Evening Bulletin* and *Philadelphia Daily News*, his Philadelphia career spanned 46 years.

His broadcasting career began on April 9, 1963, as he joined By Saam and Bill Campbell. Eight years later he and Kalas became a team in the booth. Kalas was the expert play-by-play announcer while "Whitey" Ashburn had

Richie Ashburn (center) began his broadcasting career with the Phillies in 1963, joining Bill Campbell (left) and By Saam (right).

the folksy, storytelling approach. His dry wit and farm-boy charm delighted millions of listeners and viewers.

Ashburn almost wasn't a Phillie as the Chicago Cubs and Cleveland Indians thought they had signed him out of Tilden, Nebraska. But MLB voided the contracts, and the Phillies signed him in 1944 for a $3,500 bonus. Philadelphia signed him as a catcher, and he made his pro debut in the minors at that position but was moved to center field during the 1945 season. During spring training in 1948, he played some games at third base and opened the season in left field because the incumbent, Harry Walker, was the defending NL batting champion. He soon replaced Walker and became one of the elite center fielders in the majors. Ashburn started his last game for the Mets at second base on September 30, 1962. He got his last hit (a ground-ball single) in the eighth inning that day.

Like all kids I tried to get autographs when I went to Shibe Park. I never got Ashburn's. Players had to walk across a concourse filled with fans to get from the clubhouse to the runway to the dugout. Ashburn always walked in the middle of tall pitchers, making him inaccessible.

After joining the Phillies, I mentioned that to him. "You were probably one of those brats who always tried to get autographs," he joked. I also told him Ennis was my hero. Ashburn asked why. I replied, "Del drove in all those runs." He bristled, "Well, who do you think was on base all the time?"

When we retired his number in 1979, my "back porch idea" had him walk in from center field, his All-Star position. The podium would be at home plate because he was a two-time batting champion. As he began walking in from beyond the center-field fence, I thought, *Oh, boy, that's a long walk.* As Ashburn got closer, his facial expression was not one of glee. Following the ceremonies he and I got in the press elevator. "Baron," he said, "that was the dumbest thing I've ever seen, making me walk from center field. Whose stupid idea was that?" "Whitey, you are looking at that person," I said meekly. "Well, Baron, that's your dumbest moment." When you were around Ashburn, you laughed a lot. Not this time.

While he always wore No. 1 with the Phillies, others who wore that number after he was traded included coach Al Vincent (1961–63), coach George

Myatt (1964–68), manager Bob Skinner (1969), manager Frank Lucchesi (1970–72), coach Carroll Beringer (1973–77), and outfielder Jose Cardenal (1978–79). The night we retired his number, he again bristled. "You finally retired my number," he said, "and gave me a Jose Cardenal jersey." As you can tell, Ashburn was a competitor whether he was playing golf, tennis, ping pong, or cards. And he didn't hold back on his opinions.

The Baseball Hall of Fame called me in spring training of 1995. The Veterans Committee announcement was scheduled on a Tuesday afternoon that February. A couple of days later, the call so many of us waited for so long finally arrived. The Hall of Fame called, asking for his phone number and whether I could bring him to Tampa for a press conference. I had alerted Ashburn of the Hall of Fame announcement schedule. Once again, he bristled. "What makes you think I'll get in? I haven't had a hit in 32 years," he said. This time he got the good news. We went to Tampa and then headed back to Clearwater. He was appreciative but still steaming that it took this long. "Baron, I just may not go to Cooperstown," he said. "What do you think of that?" I responded, "Whitey, if you don't go, you will be robbing your family of the greatest day of their lives." Silence ensued. "Well," he said, "I guess you are right."

When it came to the induction day in Cooperstown, Ashburn delivered a speech straight from his heart and without a script. Among the 20,000-plus were numerous family members, including his 91-year-old mother. "Another great thing, I get to go in with Schmitty," he said. "Now you don't plan something like this. You can't orchestrate it. Mike, of course, is going in on the first ballot. I am going in 30-some years after I retired. Nobody could ever plan anything like that."

He ended by recalling his last play as a player, being the third out of a triple play as the Mets lost (a record 120th game) at Wrigley Field. "As we walked into the clubhouse, Casey Stengel was standing there, and he said to us, 'Fellas, I don't want anybody to feel bad about this. This has been a real team effort. No one or two people could have done this.' Well, I'm going to quote Casey. No one or two people could have done all this today. And everybody that had a part of it, God bless, and especially the fans, you have made this the greatest day of my life."

The year after his induction, my wife Julie was involved in a car accident on Labor Day, in which a pickup truck hit her vehicle's front left side. It was a pretty good fender bender. She wasn't taken to the hospital, but she sustained an injured right shoulder. That night I had dinner with Ashburn in the press club and mentioned the accident. I went to my office during the game and heard Ashburn say on television: "We want to send along our best to Ruly Carpenter. Ruly was in a car accident." (He proceeded to describe Julie's accident to a tee.) After that half inning, I went into the booth, "Whitey, where did you get that story about Ruly?" I asked. "Someone told me in the press club tonight," he said. "Whitey, that someone was me, and it was Julie and *not Ruly*." He paused and came back as only he could: "Well, you need to speak more clearly."

When the game resumed, Ashburn reported: "We were given some mis-information about Ruly and a car accident. It was Julie Shenk." Meanwhile, Ruly was getting calls from his friends, wanting to know if he was alright. The following spring training, Julie had her right shoulder in a sling after surgery. "Juls, what happened to you?" Ashburn asked. Julie told him the accident story, and he responded, "Why doesn't anybody ever tell me these things?"

I unearthed more stories in 1988 when we were honoring Ashburn for his 40 years in the game. I sat down with him to write a Baron's Corner with the hopes of promoting the special night. Ashburn had some great anecdotes.

- "As a kid in Tilden, Nebraska, there wasn't much to do but play sports. I loved to run and I could run like a deer. My twin sister, Donna, was the only person who could give me a run for the money. We used to run races in county fairs for prize money. Either she or I would win."
- "The first big league game I ever saw, I played in, against the Boston Braves at Connie Mack Stadium. My first major league hit was a single off Johnny Sain."
- "Robin Roberts was my first roommate at the old Phoenix Hotel in Clearwater, spring training of 1948, my first spring training. I had a lot of roommates along the way...Putsy Caballero, Ron Northey—when he snored the room shook—Granny Hamner, Don Zimmer [with the Cubs] and Frank Thomas [with the Mets]. Putsy and I roomed

together at Utica. We used to tease Stan Lopata all the time. One day Stan came bursting into our room, picked up both of us—one in each arm—and took us to the window. We were 13 stories up, and he threatened to drop us unless we quit picking on him. We got the message."

- "The schedule was different when I played. Mondays and Thursdays were travel days. We played doubleheaders almost every Sunday. Why one year, I played in 35 doubleheaders. We'd travel by train. I loved it. Great times. We had our own car and dining room. Cooking was elegant. The team lived together, played cards, talked a lot of baseball. Very relaxing."
- "In the late 1950s, the Phillies took my Cadillac away from me and gave me a new one. It turned out to be a lemon. That winter I was in Mobridge, South Dakota. It stopped dead. Last time I've ever seen it. That wasn't the end. That winter I got a notice from the IRS that I owed $2,800 in taxes on the car, which was given to me as a gift. So, do me a favor, don't give me a car."

On September 9, 1997, GM Ed Wade called early in the morning with the shocking news that Ashburn had died in a New York hotel. I'll never forget Ashburn's memorial service. Over 40,000 people passed by his casket at Memorial Hall. They came dressed in suits and cutoffs, young and old, rich and poor, from nearby and far away. The blind were there. One fan left a small transistor by his casket. The entire Phillies team came in uniform to pay their respects. Fans piled flowers by his Wall of Fame plaque at the Vet.

Jim Bunning (1996)

Bunning was the hardest working pitcher I've been around. During batting practice pitchers would run from foul pole to foul pole along the warning track. Conditioning the legs was key in pitching. He'd run and run in spring training and also between starts. He was all business as a player and very active in the player's association. If the club violated some of the rules in the basic agreement, he would speak up *quickly*.

43

Bunning wound up in our uniform twice. He won the first game at Veterans Stadium, came back to throw out the first ball on the 10th anniversary in 1981 and again in 2001, the day we officially retired his number. He did the same in 2003 during the final opener in Veterans Stadium history. That has to be a record for most ceremonial first pitches.

When inducted into the Hall of Fame, players have some say as to the cap to be displayed on their plaque. Bunning didn't hesitate; he chose the Phillies. He's said many times that we pay attention to our former players better than any club. His induction speech was lengthy and filled with messages and vintage Bunning anecdotes. Two years earlier baseball had canceled the World Series because of a strike. "To the fans today, I would like to say: you made baseball our national sport," he said. "Please don't give up on it now. To the owners, get your house in order. Figure out how you want to share your revenues without going to the players and asking them to foot the bill. Get an agreement with the players, a long-term agreement, a minimum of 10 years. To the owners and players alike, get a commissioner. A real commissioner! Come up with a way to mutually share the cost of the commissioner's office and mutually hire, if necessary through a third party, a real commissioner with restored powers of that office prior to 1950. To the players, realize your obligations as professional athletes and look beyond your contractual obligations and accept the fact that you also have an obligation and duty to the game of baseball and to yourselves as human beings to conduct yourselves as gentlemen at all times and in the best interest of the game. No one person is bigger than the game itself." He ended as did his friend, Ashburn, by saying, "You have made this the best day of my life."

Minor league manager and player agent were given a try after he took off the uniform. He then entered politics, climbing from being a city councilman in Fort Thomas, Kentucky, to state senator, to the U. S. House of Representatives, and a two-term U. S. Senator. He retired from his political career in 2010.

He and his wife, Mary, have nine children and 35 grandchildren. While visiting spring training in Clearwater in 2013, ESPN taped an interview with him at Bright House Field. The network was interviewing perfect game pitchers. While leaving the park, Jim and Mary walked through the merchandise store. Mary spotted a Phillie Phanatic doll. She beamed. "Jim, isn't this cute?" "Careful Mary," he replied, "You have to buy 44 of them."

Harry Kalas (2002)

Sitting in the third base dugout at Connie Mack Stadium in 1965, a blond person was walking toward our dugout. Mauch leaned over and asked, "Baron, who is this guy coming toward us?" I responded, "I'm not sure of his name, but he is with Houston's broadcasting team, although he sits in the press box most of the game." Turns out the person was young Harry Kalas in his first year as part of the Houston Astros radio broadcasting team of Gene Elston and Loel Passe. He did one just inning per game that season.

When Bill Giles came to Philadelphia, one of his first moves was to hire Kalas. It was a very unpopular move because Kalas was replacing legendary broadcaster Campbell. Giles made a lot of great contributions to the Phillies and the city. Bringing Kalas in was one of his best moves. Kalas teamed with Saam and Ashburn initially. Eventually, he and Ashburn became the most beloved sports broadcasters the city has ever known.

When Veterans Stadium opened in 1971, Kalas was the emcee for the pregame festivities. He forgot to introduce Chub Feeney, National League president, among the many dignitaries that were on the field. We used to laugh about that often. His first Phillies broadcast was that day, and years later he was the emcee for the closing ceremonies of the Vet and then the opening ceremonies at Citizens Bank Park. Unpopular at the beginning, that changed over time, a complete 180-degree change. He loved the fans, and it showed. He never missed being part of the caravan. He made appearances during the offseason and also became the voice of NFL Films.

One year our caravan left the Vet early on a Tuesday morning. As he had done for years, Kalas emceed the Philadelphia Sports Writers Association banquet, which was held on Monday night. The writers had a hospitality room open after the banquet, and the parties went on and on. Knowing he had the caravan the next morning, Kalas decided to stay at the Holiday Inn near the Vet. I heard that before going to bed he asked the operator to leave a wake-up call for him at 6:30 AM. His watch had stopped, so he then asked the operator the present time. She said it was 6:15.

Harry loved Mike Schmidt—MICH-el Jack Schmidt—as only he could say. Another favorite was Mi-ckey Mor-an-DI-ni. During my traveling days, I loved stirring the pot by telling Kalas that Expos third baseman Bob Bailey was a better player than Schmidt. He'd get hot and tell me, "You don't know what you are talking about." Imagine having that statement aimed at you in that powerful and distinctive voice of his. The signature call of that voice was, "That ball's outta here." Nobody could match his voice and excitement.

Many a night, I left Veterans Stadium late after a game. Kalas would be standing by his car signing autograph after autograph. He never cut the fans short. How popular were Kalas and Ashburn? During the 1980 World Series, Phillies broadcasters were not allowed to call the games. MLB had contracts with NBC and CBS Radio that kept local broadcasters off the air. But the fan upheaval was so strong that Major League Baseball changed the policy after that World Series.

The Phillies universe went into shock when the stunning news came out of New York City that Ashburn had died. Kalas kept on going, though a part of him had been taken away. In 2002 he received the prestigious Ford C. Frick Award for "major contributions to baseball" during Hall of Fame ceremonies in Cooperstown. Seven years earlier on the same stage, Ashburn was inducted into the shrine. Once again Phillies fans flocked to the New York village for the ceremonies. We had a large contingent of executives and buses of office staff there. We had a party in a tent to celebrate the event and honor Kalas. He performed his "High Hopes" rendition at the party, and everybody was singing along.

Kalas was deeply touched by the honor and prepared a poem for the occasion:

This is to the Philadelphia fan
To laud your passion as best I can
Your loyalty is unsurpassed
Being the Fightin's in first or last
We come to the park each day

Looking forward to another fray
Because we know you'll be there
We know you really care
You give opposing pitchers fits
Because as one loyalist shouts, "Everybody hit!"
To be sure, in Philadelphia there might be some boos
Because you passionate fans, like the manager, hate to lose
Your reaction to the action on the field that you impart
Spurs us as broadcasters to call the game with enthusiasm and heart
We feel your passion through and through
A Philadelphia fan, I love you.

I remember asking Harry one winter, "Do you think you will ever retire?" He answered quickly, "No, what would I do?" Kalas broadcast the 1983 and 1993 World Series, but both times the Phillies failed to win a world championship. But that all changed in 2008 when the Phillies defeated the Tampa Bay Rays in six games. With Chris Wheeler pumping his fists in the background and not saying a word, Kalas let it fly when Lidge struck out Eric Hinske. "The Philadelphia Phillies are 2008 world champions of baseball," he declared. We'll never forget that call.

The following April he called a Matt Stairs home run in Coors Field, Denver, on a Sunday afternoon. Never did anyone ever think that would be his last "outta here" call. Preparing for the game in the visiting TV booth at Nationals Park in Washington the next day, he collapsed and died. "We lost our voice," David Montgomery said.

When word came that Kalas had died, fans immediately began laying flowers at the base of the Schmidt statue. His memorial service took place at Citizens Bank Park with the casket at home plate. The service concluded when his casket was passed along by friends, broadcast partners, and former and current players before it was placed in a hearse. Kalas then left Citizens Bank Park for the last time.

For years Ashburn and Kalas entertained us in living rooms, on porches, in cars, at the beach, or while we sat on a park bench. They were like family members. When Ashburn died, the Phillies won the next game 1–0 against the Mets. Ashburn wore No. 1 and last played for the Mets. When Kalas died, the Phillies won the next game 9–8 against the Nationals. Amazingly, Ashburn's last broadcast was September 8 (9/8).

Harry had always been the emcee for the Toyota Wall of Fame ceremonies. Even after his passing, Dan Stephenson in the video department was able to use a recording of Kalas introducing the Wall of Famers. Eventually, we had to change plans.

Through a group of fans, funding was raised for a Kalas statue. The unveiling came on August 16, 2011, the fifth statue at Citizens Bank Park. The Schmidt, Carlton, and Roberts statues are located at gates outside the park. Kalas' is inside the park about 300 feet from Ashburn's statue—just where it should be.

Pat Gillick (2011)

I was so pleased when we hired Gillick. Hey, we had somebody who was near my age! Plus his track record was simply outstanding. Wherever he went he took his team to the postseason, which we hadn't done since 1993. Gilllick was a lot like Owens, a grass roots baseball man who loved the scouting and player development phase of the game. Both played minor league baseball, never got to the majors, and began their off-the-field careers as scouts before moving into the GM world.

Gillick was a left-handed pitcher for the University of Southern California team that won the 1958 College World Series. He turned pro the following year and spent five seasons in the Baltimore Orioles system, compiling a 45–32 record with a 3.42 ERA in 164 games (98 starts). Along the minor league trail, he played against several young Phillies prospects. He remembered them and their teams: "Dick Allen in Williamsport and Little Rock; John Boozer in Des Moines and Chattanooga; Lee Elia in Chattanooga; John Herrnstein, Fergie Jenkins, and Danny Cater in Little Rock; Ray Culp in Des Moines and Williamsport; Dennis Bennett and Pat Corrales in Bakersfield." He knew the managers, too: "Andy Seminick managed Des Moines in 1960,

Frank Lucchesi had Williamsport in 1962, and Paul 'the Pope' Owens in Bakersfield in 1959."

Gillick started his post-playing career as a scout, and that side of the game never left him. He had a simple philosophy as GM. "You don't have to be the smartest person to excel," Gillick said. "You can always outwork the other guy." He believed in building through the farm system. Statistics are important, but there is more than numbers. You have to see the player and you have to see him on the field, how he plays the game," Gillick said. "Is he intense? Does he have passion? Get his body language. See how he interacts with the other players on the team. When I started I thought it was 70 percent ability and 30 percent character. And the longer I've been in it, I think it is 60 percent character and 40 percent ability. Good character people help a team pull through the difficult times."

When he joined us, he didn't make the sweeping changes, which often occurs with a new GM. Instead he worked with those in scouting and player development and began grooming Ruben Amaro Jr. for the role. Baseball 24/7 is his style. He remembers everything and does it without a pen and pad. When he hears a phone number or a name for the first time, it is locked in his memory bank. I don't remember the particular player we had acquired, but I was in his office talking about bringing the player to Philadelphia. "There's a flight on US Air, No. 2314 that leaves L.A. at 2:30 PM," Gillick said. He wasn't looking at a book or the computer. He just knew it. His attention to detail was incredible. "We're in St. Louis and Pat, the GM then, called me for some information on one of our players," said Greg Casterioto, our director of baseball communications. "At the end of the conversation, Pat asked me, 'What room are you in?' I told him 221. He replied, 'You're near the elevator then and hung up.' I sat there for a minute or two and wondered how did he know that."

Gillick's persona is a man who listened to his scouts and staff, a man who is warm and friendly, a man who would laugh heartily, a man who could pick your brain. He is very friendly and caring, but he could pass you in the hallway as if you didn't exist. Gillick could agitate with the best and was always on the run. He could be in the office one day and in an airplane the next day going to scout a player. When pursuing a free agent, his style was to get on a plane and have a face-to-face visit. When going after a trade, he was imaginative, focused, and realistic. In his three-year stint with us, we went from second place to the division championship to being the world champions.

When Pat was inducted into the Hall of Fame, Montgomery summed up Gillick perfectly. "Whether you were an area scout in Oregon or a pro scout covering the big leagues or following the South Atlantic League, he had time for everybody and he always knew what you were doing," Montgomery said. "He was a great listener and had the unique ability to make everyone around him better."

His speech in Cooperstown was thoughtful and sincere and vintage Gillick. As could be expected, he thanked a lot of people but modestly said, "My particular thanks go to the scouts and player development staff. They find the players and prepare them for Major League Baseball. The hard work, dedication, and advice from scouts and player development staff are what build champions."

He made another comment that really stuck with me. "Baseball is about talent and hard work and strategy, but at the deepest level it's about love, integrity, and respect," he said. "Respect for the game, respect for your colleagues, respect for the shared bond that is bigger than any one of us." We thought the message was so powerful, we printed a color image of Gillick making his acceptance speech and added his quote at the bottom of the 8"x10" print. Every employee received a copy.

CHAPTER 3
HOMEGROWN LEGENDS

When the Whiz Kids won the 1950 pennant, the core of the team—Robin Roberts, Richie Ashburn, Del Ennis, Curt Simmons, Willie Jones, Granny Hamner, Andy Seminick, Stan Lopata, and Bob Miller—was homegrown. Because of their youth, they were named the "Whiz Kids," but they never repeated as champions. The best they did was a third-place finish three years later.

Along came another core—Mike Schmidt, Larry Bowa, Greg Luzinski, Bob Boone, Dick Ruthven, Keith Moreland, Lonnie Smith, Larry Christenson, and Marty Bystrom—that came up through the farm system in the 1970s. That group won three straight division titles, starting in 1976 but always failed to reach the World Series. That frustration ended when the Phillies won their first World Series championship in 1980. A repeat in 1981 was aborted in the strike-shortened, split season.

The scouting department and player development produced another core that dominated the National League by appearing in five consecutive post-seasons from 2007 to 2011. Included was a world championship (2008) and a return to the Fall Classic the following year, the first back-to-back World Series in our history. This core included Jimmy Rollins, Chase Utley, Ryan Howard, Pat Burrell, Cole Hamels, Carlos Ruiz, Kyle Kendrick, and Brett Myers. It is the greatest era in our history. Had a second wild-card been in play in 2005 and 2006, we would have had two more postseason appearances. The core of that core is Rollins, Utley, and Howard—three players with exceptional talent. They are stars who dominated the top of the batting order. Rollins and Utley have played the most games of any shortstop-second base combination among active players.

Rollins, a native of Oakland, California, wound up as our second-round selection in 1996. He has proven he *can* play in the big leagues as our scout, Bob Poole, had stated in his report. Another switch-hitter from northern California, Bowa, was considered the Phillies greatest shortstop until Rollins came along. During J-Roll's pro debut at Martinsville, Virginia, he averaged .238 in 49 games, the lowest he's had for any season. Arriving in the big leagues in 2000, he began to put up numbers that continue to grow. He became the first shortstop in major league history to make the All-Star team the first two years in the majors. Rollins ended 2005 with a 36-game hitting streak, the longest single-season streak in our history. He extended it two more games the next season. Rollins and Utley became the first middle infielders in baseball history with 25 or more home runs that year. In 2007 Rollins became the first player in major league history to collect at least 200 hits, 15 triples, 25 homers, and 25 stolen bases in one season. In 2008 he went on the disabled list for the first time. In his first game back, he went 3-for-5, including a two-run homer and an RBI double. He's considered the player that makes the Phillies go. Rollins is often referred to as a "red light player," meaning he performs the best when there's a big stage. Among the Phillies all-time top 10 hitting categories, Rollins' name appears as often and as high on the charts as Hall of Fame third baseman Mike Schmidt. Interestingly, both were second-round selections.

Coming out of UCLA, Utley was a second baseman, though some scouts felt he should move to third base. He tried that at Scranton-Wilkes-Barre, Pennsylvania, but returned to his natural position, second base, in his third pro season (2003) and made the Phillies Opening Day roster. Sent back to the minors after one at-bat (an April 4 strikeout), he returned 20 days later in grand fashion. That afternoon he got his first major league hit, a grand slam home run. He ended the season by grounding into a double play as the last batter in the history of Veterans Stadium. Utley came close to matching Rollins' club-record hitting streak with a 35-game streak in 2006. The next season he went on the DL for the first time with a broken right hand. He once again made a triumphant return. On August 27 he made a curtain call after going 3-for-5 with a home run and RBI double. Utley certainly has a flair for the dramatic. On Opening Day in 2013, Utley hit the 200th home run of his career.

Of course, Phillies fans will always remember his 2009 World Series performance, even though Philadelphia lost to the New York Yankees. He had a pair of two-homer games, including going deep twice in the first post-season game played in the new Yankee Stadium. He finished the series with five homers, matching Reggie Jackson's record. In an interview with politico.com, former U.S. president and former Texas Rangers owner George W. Bush even said Utley would be the first player he would select if he were still an

MLB team owner. That was 2008. The next season *The Sporting News'* list of the 50 greatest current players in baseball ranked Utley sixth. During that December *Sports Illustrated* named Utley as the second baseman on its All-Decade Team. His work ethic and preparation is off the charts. He arrives early every day and spends hours watching video and hitting. One writer referred to him as the gym rat of the video room. In the dugout his eyes are always focused on the pitcher. Utley doesn't say much. His actions on the field say everything. Many consider Utley the heart and soul of the team that dominated for so many seasons. As Harry Kalas once said, "Chase Utley, you are the man."

Howard's Southwest Missouri State College career numbers were numbing: 50 home runs, 183 RBIs, .335 average in 172 games. He was nicknamed "the Big Hurt" and had his uniform number retired. Once he reached the big leagues, Charlie Manuel named him "the Big Piece." With Jim Thome anchored at first base, we tried playing him in the outfield. Like Utley, Howard returned to his normal position. Other clubs had called general manager Ed Wade, hoping to pry Howard away, but it was Thome, who was eventually dealt.

Howard put up staggering home run numbers. He was the fastest ever to reach 100, 150, 200, and 250 homers, passing Hall of Famer Ralph Kiner each time. His first home run came off a New York Mets pitcher who is not exactly a household name, Bartolome Fortunato, on 9/11/04. In 2006 he became the first player to hit a home run into Ashburn Alley at Citizens Bank Park and the first to hit one into the third deck in right field. Dick Allen hit the longest homers in Connie Mack Stadium, and Greg Luzinski did the same at Veterans Stadium. Howard quickly acquired the same distinction in a ballpark that was just two years old. Howard finished with 58 long balls that season, surpassing Thome's club record (47) for a first baseman and Mike Schmidt's overall club high (48).

During the early part of their careers, many media envisioned MVP Awards and induction into the Baseball Hall of Fame and Museum in Cooperstown, New York, for Rollins, Utley, and Howard. Howard and Rollins were MVPs in 2006 and 2007, respectively. Plaques in Cooperstown for Utley and Howard were scratched as both faced serious injuries since we last appeared in the postseason (2011). Rollins is putting up Hall of Fame numbers. If he stays healthy, those numbers can go higher. There is no doubt each will be inducted in our Wall of Fame. The skills of this very potent trio are different. Rollins is a five-tool player, Utley excels as a bear-down hustler, and Howard is the power-hitting cleanup hitter. They are clubhouse leaders in different ways.

We hold media training with players early in their big league careers. Here they are also different. Rollins can be hot and cold in dealing with the media. Of the three he's more prone to provide a quote that grabs head-lines, such as his preseason quote in 2007: "The Mets had a chance to win the World Series last year. Last year is over. I think we are the team to beat in the National League East finally—but on paper." Writers had a ball with that quote. Often his last quote "on paper" was omitted, which made for a better story. Next year Rollins predicted the Phillies would win 100 games. We won 92 in the regular season and 11 in the postseason. Utley was very attentive during the media training and very inquisitive, asking a lot of questions. He recognizes the importance of media availability after games but is very guarded in his comments. Well, he was guarded until the Citizens Bank Park celebration that ended the World Series parade in 2008. He stepped to the microphone and proclaimed, "World Champions. World [Bleeping] Champions!" Howard is a stand-up guy with the media and is generally available day-in and day-out, both pre and postgame. He was a communications major in college, and that may have something to do with it. Of the trio Howard has done more commercial appearances, including his nationally known Subway advertisements.

When their playing days are over, Rollins, Utley, and Howard will be universally recognized as the greatest players at their respective positions in our history. They've already hit the most home runs in club history (single-season and career) at their positions. In the community all three have been extremely active with charitable events. Each supports the other's events. Three different drafts produced three players who became fixtures at the top of the order. It will be a long, long time until someone matches the careers of No. 11, 26, and 6.

COLLECTIVE NUMBERS OF THE BIG TRIO

1	Rookie of the Year
1	NLCS MVP Award
2	MVP Awards
4	Gold Glove Awards
6	Silver Sluggers
6	NL Player of the Month
10	All-Stars
13	NL Player of the Week
13	Trips to the DL
727	Home Runs
975	Doubles
2,603	RBIs
2,794	Runs Scored
4,453	Games
4,761	Hits

CHAPTER 4
BALLPARKS

Shibe Park/Connie Mack Stadium

Getting to Shibe Park from Myerstown, Pennsylvania, in the 1940s meant taking Route 422 through Reading, Pottstown, and Norristown to Henry Avenue in Roxborough. There was a certain spot on Henry Avenue where you got the first glimpse of the Shibe Park light towers. That became a landmark of excitement every time. Many years later, 1965 to be specific, my wife, Julie, and I moved from Wilmington to Roxborough, and Henry Avenue became a daily route.

There was nothing like the buzz of the ballpark once the gates opened. A quiet place became alive. Fans streamed in the gates and filled the ground-level concourse. You could hear vendors selling scorecards, saying, "Get your scorecard right here!" The smell of hot dogs and popcorn filled the air. There were no elevators or escalators. To get from one level to another, you had to climb stairs. A box seat sold for $2.25. The seats were wooden, and the aisles were narrow. The concrete was soiled from all the years. I loved to roam the entire park. During one of my roams, I came across the legendary Connie Mack and another gentleman sitting in the mezzanine section behind home plate. As I approached Mr. Mack, the other person motioned to stay away. Mr. Mack motioned otherwise. He kindly signed an autograph.

Kenny Bush was the Phillies bat boy and he used to take infield practice with the second unit. I was envious. But at first I was bothered, too, because the players clowned around before the games. Why aren't they taking this serious? Once in the game, I learned that having fun was necessary to maintain your spirits during the long grind of the season.

For those observing that grind, the press box was mounted pretty high up under the upper deck roof. My seat was right in the middle, and I had a great bird's-eye view of the field. The elevator that took us to the top level was tiny and slow. Four people, maybe five, could fit, if everyone inhaled at the same time. Games at Connie Mack Stadium started at 8 PM. From late afternoon until game time seemed like an eternity. On a few occasions, I shagged during batting practice. The press box had a tiny kitchen that featured sandwiches and hot dogs for every home game. Dick Young, a highly respected New York baseball columnist, asked for a hot dog. He was handed a paper plate with a hot dog. He complained loudly, "Where's the roll?" The attendant replied, "You didn't ask for a roll."

Once the game started, my job didn't seem like work. I was being paid to watch a baseball game. Sitting in the press box, keeping score, researching records, handling media questions, and making announcements over the press box PA was the ritual. Though it was fun, there was one very scary moment at the old place, the last game on October 1, 1970. Through Bill Giles' leadership, we had big plans to close the place. All fans received a certificate, saying they saw the last game at Connie Mack Stadium. As a commemorative souvenir to fans, 5,000 wooden slats that were used to repair the seats were given away. During the game fans began banging the slats in an effort to take home other souvenirs. Suddenly, we had the world's loudest drum. "The sound of chopping with the seat slats is a definite memory," said Tony Siegle, the director of stadium operations back then. "We had police guarding the offices, which is the one area the marauders didn't get to. I remember huddling on the field along the fence in the seventh inning with some of our staff. We knew then all hell was going to break loose. We had postgame plans to dig up home plate, have a helicopter land, and take home plate to Veterans Stadium. We were going to give away autographed uniform stuff, but all of that went by the boards. Once the game ended, fans stampeded the field. We had to cancel the helicopter, but we saved home plate from being taken, protected the offices, and locker rooms. Everything else seemed to be fair game. Urinals were carried out of the place. Fans scooped up clumps of dirt from the field like thousands of front end loaders. The wooden left-field wall was stripped. Heck, fans came armed with hammers, wrenches, and saws—frightening."

While Siegle was in the war zone, I was still in the press box. It began to shake, something I had never experienced before. That was also frightening. Thank goodness we won the game in extra innings with Tim McCarver scoring on an Oscar Gamble single. Otherwise, we might have had a full riot on our hands. Leaving Connie Mack Stadium wasn't painful. The place was rundown, antiquated. Despite a nice playing field, parking and other amenities for the fans were terrible. The playing field was excellent, the only plus. Yes, a lot of history took place in the grand old place, involving the A's, Phillies, and Eagles.

We had our first Old-Timers' Game at Veterans Stadium on August 21, 1971. As we were unveiling the statue of Connie Mack that was moved from across the street at Connie Mack Stadium to the corner of Broad Street and Pattison Avenue, word came that the old ballpark had caught fire. Eerie!

CONNIE MACK STADIUM/SHIBE PARK MEMORIES

Larry Bowa "[I] played my first big league game there. I thought it was the Taj Mahal. The neighborhood was a little scary. The guard would not let me in. I told him I was a member of the Phillies, but he didn't believe me. I thought it was a great park as far as the playing surface. It was a great experience to play there."

Clay Dalrymple "[I] enjoyed playing there. It was a fun, interesting, and unique place. Measurements were like no other place. That right-field wall was enticing, but the height meant you had to really hit it to get a home run. Then there was that big clock on top of the scoreboard. For a home run, you had to hit it *over* the clock. My first big league game was there, second game of a Sunday doubleheader. Don Newcombe was pitching for the Reds. He struck me out the first time, but then I had consecutive doubles in my next two at-bats."

Tommy Lasorda "I remember going to a game at Shibe Park when I was 15 to 16 years old, bought a program for 10 cents, and waited outside the New York Giants clubhouse on the first-base side of the park. I wanted to get some autographs just like any normal kid. Players had to walk across the concourse to get to the dugout. A player came out, and I asked for his autograph. He shoved me aside. I looked at his number in the program. Buster Maynard was his name. Well five to six years later, I'm pitching in the Sally League against Augusta. [I] retired the first two batters when I heard, 'Now batting, Buster Maynard.' I thought it is time to get even. First two pitches nearly hit him. He barked at me not to do that again, so I drilled him, and we had a fight. After the game, I'm leaving the clubhouse when this guy in a suit comes to me,

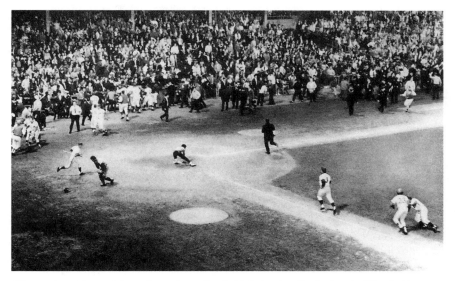

Players head for safety as fans storm the field, following the last out of the final game at Connie Mack Stadium in 1970.

'You Lasorda?' I nodded yes. 'I'm Buster Maynard.' I said, "If you want to have it out right here, let's go.' He said, 'No, I want to know why you threw at me.' I told him the story, he shook his head, and walked away. I remembered that day at Shibe Park and how I felt. I always tried to be the opposite and told my players the same.

Bob Miller "I was called up from Terre Haute in 1949 on a day off for the Phillies, roomed with Robin Roberts. He and Curt Simmons invited me to go to Shibe Park to get in some running and hopefully find some baseballs, so we could throw. I was in awe of Shibe Park. [I] never dreamed that I would ever be in a big league park. I thought it was a great place to play. Fans were close to the players. I loved the place."

Tony Taylor "Best park I ever played in. As a hitter you could see the ball well. As an infielder the infield was the best in the game. Fans were close to the field. You could hear them and talk to them. It was like a family affair."

Bob Uecker "The place was old, everything. The field was the best. Center field seemed like 1,000 feet away. [I] wish today's players, who have all kinds of fancy amenities, could have experienced Connie Mack Stadium...small clubhouse, trainer's room on second floor, no beer, no food, no doors on the johns. It was a place to get dressed for a game. Catching once a week can wear your body down. [I] climbed the steps to the trainer's room and went in the whirlpool. [The] trainer asked if I wanted to listen to the radio. 'Sure.' He threw the radio into the whirlpool. [I] got the idea that they didn't want me around anymore."

Bobby Wine "[I] played my first game in the majors there. Roberto Clemente made a sliding catch to rob me of a hit in my first at-bat. While the clubhouse facilities were awful, the playing field was awesome. I also played in the last game there with the Expos, hit a double, a game-tying hit in the ninth. As soon as the Phillies won in the 10th, fans stormed the field. It was scary getting to the safety of the clubhouse."

Veterans Stadium

The groundbreaking took place on October 2, 1967. Because of design changes, labor strikes, bad weather, grand jury probes, and political infighting, the construction schedule was delayed. A 1970 opening was postponed one year. A chilly, windy April 10, 1971, was Opening Day for our new home, Veterans Stadium. Jim Bunning, the oldest starting pitcher in the majors at 39 years of age, started and won his 220th game. Larry Bowa got the first hit, and Don Money hit the first home run. "It's Beautiful," was the headline in the *Philadelphia Evening Bulletin*. "It's a beautiful place," *Sports Illustrated* wrote.

The city of Philadelphia funded the new multi-purpose facility. We had limited feedback into the design. I did attend meetings the city held in deciding the location of the press box. Radio and television claimed they should be behind home plate. The Baseball Writers Association of America argued loud and long that the writers belonged in the prime seats behind home plate. A compromise was reached, and broadcasting booths were moved to the third-base side of home plate and writers to the first-base side.

The *Evening Bulletin* conducted polls for the name of the new place. Over 500 suggestions came from 1,650 readers: Philadelphia Stadium, Independence Stadium, William Penn Stadium, Eisenhower Stadium, Philadium, Pretzel Stadium, Ye Old Park, Boo-Bird Stadium, and Philadron were among the suggestions. I remember submitting two: Billy's Penn and the Playpen. City Council had the final say and selected Veterans Stadium.

Astroturf was the new fad in athletic fields. It was needed when two teams played in the same facility. Veterans had 65,000 seats, which was too large a capacity for baseball. In business you thrive on supply and demand. With that many seats, there was no demand. You could always get a seat.

We had a lot of great years in the Vet: All-Star Games, postseason games, three World Series, and jersey retirement nights. We also had wild acts and crazy promotions, including the highest jumping Easter bunny, Benny the Bomb, a cash scramble, a cow milking contest, and an ostrich race. We actually had Karl Wallenda walk across the Vet twice. Phil and Phyllis were mascots. They were part of a home run display in center field. Giles had a staff meeting every Tuesday morning in his office. That was the incubator for promotions, fun, and games. His idea was to create an atmosphere in which fans had a fun time at the ballpark no matter the outcome of the game. We all recognized that winning was the best solution to a fun time.

One of the annual promotions I enjoyed was organizing Old-Timers' Games. We had different themes, ordered uniforms from those eras, and played a three-inning game before one of the regular games. We had the likes of Hank Aaron, Willie Mays, Whitey Ford, Mickey Mantle plus many former Phillies and Philadelphia A's players. We paid for their transportation and hotel accommodations and gave them a gift. Among the gifts over the years was a Weber charcoal grill, clock radio, bumper pool table, set of drinking glasses, and a wall clock. After the games the players would sit around and reminisce about their playing days as if they didn't want to take off the uniform. Back at the hotel, I had a hospitality suite where more memories were relived. We had the 25th reunion for the 1950 Whiz Kids in 1975. They didn't receive rings for winning the 1950 pennant, so we gave the players rings. The Saturday night hospitality room at the hotel didn't end until the sun came up

Sunday morning. Russ Meyer was crying, "You don't know how much I love these guys," he said. Hours later, he was crying again, "We may never be back together again."

We started an annual photo day in which fans would be allowed on the field pregame to take close-up photos of the players, who were supposed to walk slowly. Some players didn't like this promotion and felt they were on display like animals at the zoo. Steve Carlton was one of those players. Giles would be in his press box-level box and kept track of the players who came out on the field. Every year he would call me on the dugout phone: "Baron, where's Lefty?" I'd go searching and report back to Giles, "I can't find him." To this day, Lefty won't reveal his hiding place.

In 1972 we wore blue road uniforms at home and lost 15–3 to the Atlanta Braves. That same year we were in the midst of a streak of 18 losses in 19 games. So we tried to change our luck with "Turn it Around Day." The lineup was announced in reverse order with the last names first. The seventh-inning stretch took place in the third inning. The scoreboard welcomed groups not in attendance. Ushers wore their hats backward with their nametags on their backs. It didn't help as the team dropped a 4–3 decision to the Houston Astros.

Then we wore burgundy uniforms in an effort to create some excitement in 1979. We lost that night, too, 10–5 to the Montreal Expos. Larry Christenson has the distinction of being the only starting pitcher in burgundy in our history. Though he still rags me that I mention this trivia fact, he gave me a framed photo of him in burgundy that hung in my office. While getting dressed that night, Jim Lonborg looked at Luzinski, "Bull, you look like a big grape."

In 1994 we decided to wear an alternate blue cap for all home day games. We were winless in the first three games in which they donned the blue babies. Players can be superstitious; traditionally, they like to stay in their routines. The final blow came on April 19 when the Los Angeles Dodgers rallied for a win. Coach John Vukovich came in the clubhouse after that loss and tossed his blue hat in the trash can. Vuk was known to get upset at times. A meeting of the minds on the last Friday in April settled the issue. The players volunteered to wear the blue babies for the remaining Businessperson's Specials instead of all day games. "The color of hats doesn't win or lose games," Darren

Daulton said. "Besides, the blue caps are better than the red uniforms LC told me about."

Dennis Lehman, who began his baseball career as a PR intern, went on a road trip to the West Coast in 1977 and fell in love with the San Diego chicken. He brought up the idea of a Phillies mascot at one of the staff meetings. In his book *Pouring Six Beers At A Time*, Giles said he never believed mascots would work in baseball. But he finally relented. Bonnie Erickson and Wade Harrison, who had designed Big Bird for *Sesame Street*, were contacted. "I wanted something fat, green, indefineable, and loveable," Giles said. "Their first rendition was not to my liking. I asked them to make him fatter and make his nose bigger. Adjustments were made, and Phillie Phanatic became a reality."

When Giles asked Bonnie and Wade what it would cost, they responded, "$2,900 and we own the copyright, or $5,000 and you can own the copyright." Unsure how Ruly Carpenter, then the Phillies president, would react to a $5,000 invoice for a mascot, Giles decided to save $2,100 and not purchase the copyright. "[It was the] worst mistake of my life," he said. "Years later, we had to pay $200,000 for the copyright because Phillie Phanatic had become so popular." In addition to appearing at every Phillies home game, the Phanatic made numerous other appearances. Phillie Phanatic dolls became an equally big hit.

Phillie Phanatic made its debut on April 25, 1978, before a small Vet crowd of 17,227. Jim Kaat pitched a three-hit shutout against the Chicago Cubs. The shutout got a lot more attention than the debut of this large, furry, green creature with an extendable red tongue. Being a baseball purist, I wasn't so sure. The mascot, though, won me over big time. Since his debut, the Phanatic has had two very close, inner friends, Dave Raymond and Tom Burgoyne. That's stability.

Every year one of the pre-game promotions is a Phillie Phanatic birthday party. No matter how well the team was doing on the field, this Sunday promotion filled the seats every season. All of our birthday celebrations are tied to a number that continues to grow. Somehow, the Phanatic has gotten away with not revealing his true age. I guess that's the norm in the mascot world.

But by the young or old, big or little, no matter the race, or the score of a game, the Phanatic has always been loved. No other mascot can match the universal appeal. He's been on TV shows, in movies, shared an ESPN commercial with Derek Jeter, shared a MasterCard commercial with Mr. Met, performed for presidents, traveled to foreign countries, written books, and been featured in DVDs. When you stop to think about it, no athlete can come close. That's not bad for someone who supposedly hails from the Galapagos Islands. He's even toured that Galapogos "home."

Sports Illustrated for Kids voted the Phanatic as the best mascot ever. *Forbes* magazine named him the best mascot in sports in 2008. He's one of three mascots on display in the National Baseball Hall of Fame and Museum. "From the top of his neon green head to the tip of his bubble-toed size 20 shoes, the Phillie Phanatic is every inch the best mascot in the business," USA TODAY wrote. "He's as much Philadelphia as cheesesteaks, the Liberty Bell, and Rocky Balboa. Yo, Adrian, I love dat green guy!"

Final Season

The Vet wore down. The Eagles always seemed to bash the place. We felt differently. After all it was our home for 33 years. I was asked to oversee the final season, including the closing ceremonies. It was certainly an honor, but while I was the leader, many fellow office teammates made it a successful and memorable season. The season-long celebration included players from the 1970s, 1980s, the 1993 National League champions, and wacky promotions weekends. Players were coming and going every month. Uniforms from their eras had to be ordered. The budget number had to be big, but we wanted to salute our history in the place we called home. We had a Vet countdown sign on the right-field fence, and a different person removing a number for all 81 games. The events department was kept busy with that element. I was privileged to have the honor for No. 69. The last three games were no-brainers: Carlton, Mike Schmidt, Harry Kalas. A lot of tears were shed when Harry pulled off No. 1.

The celebration ended with three games on the final weekend, September 26, 27, and 28. Prior to the last night game, we introduced our scouts and player development staffs, the men who spent endless hours trying to sign and develop winning players in the majors. After the game we had a final aerial fireworks show, and the lights were turned off for the last time.

We had a fan balloting for the All-Vet Team. Those players would be introduced prior to Saturday's day game and take their positions on the field for Sunday's closing ceremony. My idea for the All-Vet team was to dress them in something other than a baseball uniform and baseball cap. I came up with the idea of a red pinstriped tuxedo with tails and met with Mitchell & Ness Sporting Goods Company to see how creative we could be. The tux idea wasn't going to work, but Mitchell & Ness could design and manufacture a red pinstriped blazer. Without advance sizings, we had to bring a tailor to the Vet on Saturday to make last-second adjustments.

During the introduction of the All-Vet team, it began to rain lightly. Mother Nature had crashed our party with the last precipitation at the Vet. It was the last official shower in Vet history.

The stage was set for the last game and postgame closing ceremonies on Sunday, September 28. In preparation for the closing of the Vet, several of us went to Cincinnati to see the last game at Riverfront Stadium. We also looked at videos of similar events in Atlanta, Baltimore, and San Francisco. I picked up pointers from each. I also took ideas from the Opening Day ceremonies of the Winter Olympics, in which athletes paraded behind their country's flag. Along those lines Phillies alumni were introduced by the years. Flag bearers would be the front office employees with the longest tenures. Two other teams of alumni would be presented by position. Players appeared from behind home plate without public address introductions, and it was awesome. Bunning, the winning pitcher in the 1971 inaugural game, was the first alumnus to touch home plate. Before the closing ceremonies, we had to have Phillie Phanatic perform the last dance.

I had a great idea for the grand finale: Schmidt would take a final swing and circle the bases. Carlton would take the mound one more time for his final pitch, and Tug McGraw would come in from the bullpen and mime the final 1980 World Series pitch. Kalas would call each one. Talk about goose bumps. I spoke to Schmidt and Carlton early in the season to make sure they were agreeable. They were. McGraw was battling brain cancer, and we were just

Fans enjoy pregame time at one of the four statues that were located on the podium at Veterans Stadium. All four statues were refurbished by the Phillies and relocated to the parking lot where the sports facility once stood.

hoping he could be there for the ceremonies. Whatever he could do would be determined later—perhaps at the last minute.

When the alumni were getting dressed in the Eagles locker room that afternoon, Schmidt came up to me, "I've sprained my right wrist," he said. "I don't know if I can swing a bat." I pleaded, "Mike, we can't change now. Just swing with one hand." Then, Lefty said, "I can't get my arm up high enough to throw a pitch." I begged, "Then, throw it underhand." We had a limousine standing by in case McGraw couldn't make that long walk one more time. We wound up using the limo, which dropped him off at first base. McGraw made it to the mound, mimed the historic pitch that won the 1980 World Championship, and jumped into the air as best he could. It was the perfect way to close the stadium. What happened next was totally unscripted but was totally cool. All the players took a victory lap. The final ceremony was designed to provide a lasting memory and bring tears to thousands of fans, something we accomplished and Veterans Stadium deserved.

More tears flowed when on March 21, 2004, Veterans Stadium was imploded in 62 seconds. Greg Luzinski would ceremoniously push the lever that started the implosion. It would be one more Bull Blast for the Vet, but something went wrong. The implosion began before he pushed the lever. Where players had roamed and fans sat was now a huge pile of concrete and steel rubble. I'll always remember the eerie sight of the dust from the implosion drifting east over our new home.

There are so many memories of Veterans Stadium. I can still see Willie Stargell's monster home run off Bunning that landed in an exit in the 600 level in right field. Bunning said he didn't see it. "As soon as I threw it," he said, "I turned my head the other direction." Luzinski hit the most home runs (eight) into the upper deck. We kept track of every homer hit into the upper deck, Phillies and foes. Our first world championship came at 11:29 PM. We also had a game end at 4:40 AM.

ENDURING MEMORIES FROM THE VET

Bobby Abreu "The night I got my 1,000th hit."

Ruben Amaro Jr. "My first start in 1992—I had two doubles and a homer and I got a curtain call from the fans."

Larry Andersen "[The] doubleheader ending at 4:40 AM."

Bob Boone "Winning the World Series in 1980."

Larry Bowa "Tug McGraw striking out Willie Wilson to win the World Series."

Jim Bunning "[The] Opening Day win in 1971, 4–1 vs. Montreal."

Pat Burrell "Our first game back after 9/11. The pregame ceremony was awesome, and the video that Video Dan made was really emotional."

Marty Bystrom "Tug McGraw striking out Willie Wilson to win the World Series, Steve Carlton's 3,000th strikeout, Pete Rose breaking Stan Musial's all-time NL hits record."

Steve Carlton "Hiding from Bill Giles and the Baron on picture day."

Don Carman "My first game in the big leagues was in Veterans Stadium [against the Pirates], and I still remember the long jog out to the pitcher's mound. [My] second best memory—my numerous hits, but with so many, it would be hard to narrow down!"

Larry Christenson "The celebration after the final pitch when we won the World Series in 1980."

Darren Daulton "The entire 1993 season. It was a blast."

Bobby Dernier "That I started my career there and also ended it there. In addition, the two-out, three-run, inside-the-park home run in 1989."

Denny Doyle "[The] full house on Opening Day 1971! It was a great feeling!"

Jim Eisenreich "Mariano Duncan's grand slam off Lee Smith."

Jim Fregosi "There are two...the monster game that we won at four o'clock in the morning in 1993 and riding around the Vet with the National League Championship trophy after we eliminated the Braves."

Dallas Green "Easy, winning the World Series."

Tommy Greene "When we clinched the pennant in '93, and the fans [over 60,000 of them] were doing the tomahawk chop to the Braves. The stadium was rockin.'"

Greg Gross "The World Series ring ceremony in 1981."

Terry Harmon "My 18 chances at second base in 1971."

Von Hayes "Sweeping the eventual world champion Mets in 1986 to send them to St. Louis to try to clinch the Eastern Division."

Al Holland "Clinching the National League pennant against the Dodgers in 1983."

Danny Jackson "Winning playoffs at the Vet and everyone wanting the 'pump-me-up' pose."

Steve Jeltz "Hitting a home run from both sides of the plate in the same game."

Jay Johnstone "Using Larry Shenk's phone all the time...also, watching Larry Bowa beat up on the toilet when he struck out."

Ricky Jordan "Hitting a home run in my first official at-bat."

John Kruk "Game 6 NLCS, Mitch [Williams] strikes out Bill Pecota for [the] pennant. I had a great seat."

Mike Lieberthal "The night we came back to beat the Pirates in '98. We were trailing 7–1 in the bottom of the ninth inning, and I came off the bench and hit the game-winning home run. I got a standing ovation from the crowd that night. It was awesome."

Jim Lonborg "Pitching a shutout against the Cincinnati Reds the night before our daughter was born."

Frank Lucchesi "First ball thrown from helicopter to catcher Mike Ryan in 1971."

Greg Luzinski "1980 home run in first game of playoffs vs. Houston."

Garry Maddox "Winning the World Series."

Tim McCarver "Roger Freed doing sit-ups and eating chicken in the sauna; Steve Carlton's trances and excellence; Frank Lucchesi stuffing sound boxes in the clubhouse so players could not hear his show; teams from 1976, 1977, 1978, and 1980, a wealth of memories and good times."

Don Money "Hitting the first home run at the Vet."

Willie Montanez "My first home run in the big leagues; a 4-for-4 day; my first grand slam; 30 HR, 99 RBIs season; 38 doubles in a season; .304 average in a season."

Mickey Morandini "60,000 screaming fans in 1993 during our World Series run."

Dickie Noles "1980 World Series. Also my first big league game."

Mike Rogodzinski "Pinch-hit homer against St. Louis for a win in the bottom of the eighth off Diego Segui."

Jimmy Rollins "I'll never forget my first hit, which was a triple. I was just trying not to strike out. Also, the games we played against the Braves after 9/11. All those rally towels were incredible."

Mike Ryan "Catching the first ball from a helicopter on Opening Day in 1971. It's probably the highlight of my career!"

Mike Schmidt "Diving on Tug after the last out in 1980."

Kevin Stocker "July 7, 1993—20 innings in my first MLB game and winning [the] NLCS."

Kent Tekulve "Standing ovation during first appearance in Phillies uniform after 10 years of being the enemy. The fans really didn't hate me."

Tony Taylor "My 2,000th hit against the Mets."

Del Unser "One, clinching [the] '80 World Series. Two, in 1979, my third consecutive pinch-hit home run to win a game."

Chase Utley "I have three. The day I hit the grand slam as my first major league hit, [Kevin] Millwood's no-hitter, and being the last batter."

George Vukovich "Police dogs in the dugout during Game 6 of the World Series."

Mitch Williams "4:40 AM laser to left field to win the game against San Diego!"

Glenn Wilson "Being traded from Detroit to Philly in the spring of 1984 then seeing the Vet, how massive it is. Everything that came with it for my four years—the fans that came out, the media that covered the team, the people behind the scenes in the offices."

Rick Wise "September 18, 1971, vs. Cubs—[We] defeated [the] Chicago Cubs 4–3, retiring 32 straight batters from the second inning to the 12th inning and driving in the winning run in the bottom of the 12th."

Randy Wolf "My major league debut and the first game back after September 11 against the Braves."

While the Phillies were in spring training in 2004, Veterans Stadium was imploded in 62 seconds, ending 33 years as our home.

VETERANS STADIUM BIDS GOOD-BYE
By I. M. Vet

Thirty-three years ago my gates opened for the first time. Fans poured through the gates that first year and loved me, a feeling I didn't experience that much in recent years.

Through it all, millions of feet stepped on me, thousands of gallons of soda and beer were spilled on me and that yellow mustard seemed to be everywhere. I don't care if I ever see another hot dog!

Over the years, I've had several new green carpets and an order of new blue seats.

I've seen some bad baseball, good baseball, and a world championship. When Tugger struck out that Wilson fellow, I thought I would explode. I was shaking like a leaf from all the excitement.

There must have been a hundred Hall of Famers who played on my yard. There probably was another hundred that weren't here long enough for me to get to know their names.

I've seen a parade of Phillies players from Abbott to Zuber. No, there was no Costello when Abbott was here.

I've seen Wallenda walk across a wire from one side of my roof to another…twice. Boy, was I nervous.

I laughed when an Easter Bunny tried to take a hot air balloon ride out of here. Some guy named Giles thought it would be a great promotion.

Every summer I was thrilled with great aerial fireworks shows. Made me feel proud to be an American.

I've seen two All-Star Games, Presidents Nixon and Ford, and a lot of postseason games.

Those Birds from down Baltimore way once celebrated a World Series victory in my place, but that was the only time that happened.

I cried like a baby when the Phillies lost that gut-wrencher to the Dodgers in the 1977 playoffs. That one really hurt.

I've seen a game end at 4:40 in the morning on a single by Mitchie Poo, of all people. I was afraid fans were going to have breakfast at my home for the first time.

I remember crying again in 1997 when fans mourned Richie Ashburn's death. I used to listen to all the road games on radio or TV, and he really made the broadcasts entertaining.

I saw Greg Luzinski and Pat Burrell play first base when they came up from the minors. I saw Hall of Fame outfielders, Willie Mays and Hank Aaron, start games at first base late in their careers.

Seeing Juan Samuel or Lenny Dykstra run the bases for a triple really tickled me. I remember Boonie getting a triple one time. I almost fell asleep waiting for him to reach third base.

Willie Stargell made me wince when he hit that long home

run to my right field in 1972. I felt sorry for Jim Bunning that day. He didn't look after he threw the pitch. I did.

No one put on a show to my upper deck in left field better than the Bull. No one came close to Stargell in right until that Thome guy came here last year.

I don't know how many times I've heard that Kalas fellow bellow, "There's a long drive…it's outta here!" I used to get tired of hearing fans boo, but I never got tired of Harry's home run calls.

I've seen Phil and Phyllis and then the green monster, Phillie Phanatic. He made me laugh even though I saw him so often. The only thing, having a four-wheeler ride all over you sometimes got to me. But, the fans liked it and who am I to complain.

I saw the greatest retirement party ever on that last Sunday in September. To think, all those Phillies…the Bull, Schmitty, Tug, Lefty, Dutch, the Dude, Krukker, Bake, the secretary of defense, Sammy, Mickey, Eisey, LC, Dallas, the Pope and many more came back to see me one more time. Seeing them with all the guys from the '03 team was so very special.

I cried when Lefty took the mound one more time. I wept again when Schmitty circled the bases and gave Thome a high five at home plate. Then I really lost it when Tug came out of the bullpen for the last pitch.

It was a touching tribute, something I will never forget.

Now, it is time to move on. There's a new neighbor who'll house memories for millions. I saw last place in my first year. It'll be different for my new ballpark buddy in '04, I'm sure.

Citizens Bank Park

Giles started the idea that the Phillies needed their own home, an intimate baseball-only park like the Baltimore Orioles had in Camden Yards. He became chairman, paving the way for David Montgomery to become president. Under Montgomery's leadershi top-level executives; project manager John Stranix; architectural firms Ewing Cole Cherry Brott and HOK Sports; a construction management team of L. F. Driscoll and Hunt Construction group; and multiple-union workers; Citizens Bank Park became a reality. All the while, the aforementioned group was also designing and overseeing the construction of a new ballpark in Clearwater, Bright House Networks Field as it was called then. Opening two new ballparks in one year is quite an undertaking, and it was actually one month as Bright House opened on March 4, 2004, and the first game at Citizens Bank Park was on April 3.

Unlike the planning of the Vet, we had total authority in the design of our new home. There were many meetings and many arguments. Stranix oversaw the meetings. He was known to say, "Okay, we need to make a decision now. If we don't, it will affect the construction time schedule, which will affect the cost." We had toured some of the other new parks and a couple under construction during the very early planning stages. We had the opportunity to witness and learn what worked and what didn't. "If we didn't learn, then shame on us," Montgomery said.

With a 360-degree open concourse, open plaza entrances, Ashburn Alley festive entertainment area, Harry-The-K's bi-level scoreboard restaurant, a 50-foot high Liberty Bell, Bull's BBQ, "Make Your Own Phanatic" store, Phanatic play area for kids, displays of baseball history in Philadelphia—that included the Philadelphia Athletics and Negro Leagues—intimate seating, and great sightlines, our new home was "not your typical ballpark." That became our theme.

All kinds of discussion took place in designing and equipping our new home. Amenities for fans and players were at the forefront. But along came an amenity for a mascot...a bathtub. Yes, a bathtub. Phillie Phanatic had a best friend named Tom Burgoyne. At the Vet, Burgoyne would take the smelly green costume home from time to time and scrub it in his bathtub. Burgoyne's wife wasn't too enamored when the family bathroom became decorated by pieces of green fur. Burgoyne ran into Stranix. "John, my friend, the Phanatic, would love to have a bathtub in his dressing room, so he can clean his fur," he said. A somewhat bewildered Stranix offered, "We'll see." Weeks later Stranix informed Burgoyne a bathtub is now part of the plans. Previously, the only tub I ever saw at the Vet or Connie Mack Stadium was the kind filled with beer. The Phillie Phanatic used to waddle around the construction site because he couldn't drive his four-wheeler with all the piles of dirt, steel, and equipment. But I'm convinced he was just making sure his bathtub hadn't been stolen.

Debbie (Mohrdieck) Rinaldi and I oversaw the PR and multiple events, leading up to the first game in 2004. Debbie's office was located in the Preview Center, a building east of our new home that was converted from a cheese factory. Others in the building included a sales staff, receptionist, Stranix's office, and several construction staff offices. Since it was once a cheese factory, those housed in the Preview Center often reported seeing mice frolicking in the hallways. John Kruk worked for the ballclub in the sales side. His office was there, too. Kruk entertained old and new customers and the staff with his wit. The biggest attractions in the building were a model of the ballpark and a sample of a suite. Press conferences involving our new home took place there rather than the Vet, and hard hats and steel-toed boots were the daily wardrobe for months during construction.

In the middle of January 2002, excavation began. Shortly thereafter the first players—Randy Wolf, Doug Glanville, Nelson Figueroa, Mike Lieberthal, Robert Person along with manager Larry Bowa—got a look at their new home. A photo op had Glanville standing at the future site of home plate and Lieby as the catcher. "I wanted to really hit that ball," kidded Glanville, though no baseballs were being lobbed toward him. "But there was a lot of media around, and I didn't want anyone to get hurt." After all, construction workers were wearing hard hats and gloves but not baseball gloves. Pat Burrell got to swing during the taping of a Phillies commercial about the new home. Construction workers tossed balls to him, and baseballs were flying everywhere. None went over the fence simply because there was no fence yet.

The biggest press conference at the Preview Center was the signing of free-agent first baseman Jim Thome on December 6, 2002. That drew a ton of media. When leaving the center, Thome saw some electrical workers exiting the construction site. He stopped the car, got out, and chatted with the workers. As we would get to know, it was a typical gesture of a genuine person.

When word of his signing got out, over 1,000 tickets were sold that day. With Thome on board and a new home in the making, we were once again the talk of the town.

The biggest public event took place at noon on June 17, 2003, the announcement of a 25-year, $95-million naming rights agreement with Citizens Bank and the unveiling of the Liberty Bell home run celebration. The event took place in front of the red brick façade on the west side of the park and included a raised platform as the stage, media seats, TV risers, and bleachers for fans. Music was provided by the Whiz Kids band, and red and white balloons were everywhere. Montgomery and Stephen Steinour, then chairman and CEO of Citizens Bank, made the joint announcement of the naming rights. Amid confetti, streamers, and music, a hydraulic lift raised the new Citizens Bank Park sign. That was followed by the first sign to be part of the construction process, a 10' x 60' vinyl Citizens Bank Park banner unfurled from the top of the brick façade.

All four entrances to the park would eventually contain large green Citizens Bank Park signage. The first 11-ton sign was installed above the First Base Gate on February 14, 2004. (We couldn't have come up with a better partner in Citizens Bank.)

In the summer of 2003, all the employees were invited to write their names on a red steel structure that would mount the lights on the first-base side of the park. That was in the summer of 2003.

My memo to the employees:

> The Phillies are extending an invitation to each person work-ing in the front office (from veterans to interns) to be a part of Citizens Bank Park.
>
> On Monday, August 11, between 11 AM and 3 PM, you are invited to sign the steel that will be raised the next day. The piece of steel will be on a flatbed truck and will be stationed in the Taxi Lane for your convenience. Just stop by for 2 to 3 minutes and be a part of history. Special pens will be available. Feel free to bring a camera if you want to document your contribution.

PLEASE…your signature only…no love notes, hate notes, messages to mom or dad, drawings, etc.

The traveling party and all the construction workers will also have an opportunity to sign this piece of steel, which obviously is rather large.

There will be a media event on Tuesday, starting at 11:45 AM at the Third Base Gate (southwest) area to hoist the ceremonial final piece of steel to a light tower. Because of space limitations, we're asking that the staff be represented at the media event by department heads only.

When the team returned from San Francisco, in the wee hours of the morning, the buses dropped the players off at the structure, so they could sign. That event was named the "Topping Out Ceremony." Nearly 12,000 pieces of steel were erected with the final one being the autographed pieces. They were hoisted to a light tower at the southwest corner, one of the highest points of the park. Another media event was the laying of the grass in the fall of 2003. Phillies home games would be played on Mother Nature's own grass for the first time since the days of Connie Mack Stadium. One of the non-public events came late in the construction schedule, "the Great Flush." Touching, I know. Workers flushed all the toilets at the same time. Everything worked, I guess, because South Philadelphia didn't get flooded.

All the while, we and many others were putting the finishing touches on where the Vet once stood. Four statues from there were refurbished and relocated on the edges of the new parking lot. Bronze plaques on each of the four statues were needed to capture the history of events in that stadium. Markers were installed where home plate, the pitcher's rubber, three bases, and the two football goal posts once existed. And a new Veterans Memorial, located on Pattison Avenue, was designed, funded, and unveiled by the Phillies.

The On-Deck Series on April 3–4 against the Cleveland Indians, an annual two-game exhibition series, which has been played every year since Citizen Bank Park opened, served many purposes. It gave everybody—ushers, security, ARAMARK concessions, office personnel, players, and fans—a couple of dress rehearsals. It also gave us the opportunity to salute all the construction workers from the numerous unions that built the place as well as the many politicians who helped make the dream come true, a culmination of cooperation between the Phillies, the state of Pennsylvania, and city of Philadelphia.

When it came to opening ceremonies before the first National League game, there was no way we could duplicate the closing ceremonies for the Vet. That show had no clock. A pregame show, of course, is limited by time because of the upcoming game. For the opener we decided to simultaneously unveil the four statues—Hall of Famers Robin Roberts, Schmidt, Carlton, and Richie Ashburn. That was scheduled at 11 AM. Kalas joined the Ashburn family in unveiling Richie's statue. No one imagined that years later, a statue of Harry The K would become the fifth at our home.

But we still needed something unique, something that would become a tradition at Citizens Bank Park. Out of one of the weekly business staff meetings came the idea of having our players enter from the outfield, walk down 10th Street into the park past the Ashburn statue, and down a set of stairs to the field. I wasn't big on the idea. I admit I was wrong. Actually, it was similar to the start of the Phillies 1938 season when both teams marched in from center field behind a band. Baker Bowl clubhouses were in center field.

Finally, the official opener took place on April 12, 2004, vs. the Cincinnati Reds. Sitting in the press box with a great view of Center City, I couldn't believe this beautiful new place was in Philadelphia. Bobby Abreu got our first hit, a first-inning home run. The final score was 4–1, same as the Vet opener in 1971. Only that time we had the four.

Although our new home drew reviews from all directions, it was criticized because so many home runs where flying out of the place the first two years. During the first season, *The Philadelphia Inquirer* baseball writer Jim Salisbury even asked if we could measure the dimensions. So head groundskeeper Mike Boekholder, Salisbury, an *Inquirer* photographer, and I purchased several tape measures and confirmed the measurements. After viewing every home run the first two seasons, it was decided to make a physical adjustment, a project that included the relocation of the left-field wall, 22" high railing and flower

Hall of Famers Jim Bunning (left) and Robin Roberts toss the ceremonial first pitches prior to Game 5 of the 2009 World Series at Citizens Bank Park. It was Roberts' last appearance at the park before he died the following May.

beds. Two rows were removed (196 seats), which increased the wall height from 8' to 10'6". Because of those changes, home run totals became normal as time moved on. Critics had said high-profile pitchers would not come to Philadelphia to pitch in the park. Brad Lidge, Cliff Lee, and Roy Halladay would disagree.

The greatest era in Phillies history happened at the Vet, starting in 1976. Now those memories were taking a back seat to a golden era at Citizens Bank Park, which has already included five consecutive postseason appearances, including back-to-back World Series.

New attendance records were set, replacing those that were established at the Vet. The Phillies played at Shibe Park for 33-plus seasons. Only once did they ever reach 1.4 million (in 1964). Citizens Bank Park averaged more than 3.2 million during the first 10 seasons. The passion for Phillies baseball is passed on from generation to generation and from ballpark to ballpark.

CITIZENS BANK PARK INAUGURAL SEASON BY THE NUMBERS

1—First pitch, 1:32 PM, Monday, April 12, by Randy Wolf

2—Home plates, Opening Day and a new one on July 12

3—Wedding receptions

4—Full Moon home runs

6—Shutouts (four by Phillies)

7—Pounds Greg Luzinski gained at Bull's BBQ

20—Couples that got engaged

44—Sellouts

79—Third-base bags given to fans

147—Section where Jim Thome's historic 400th home run landed

186—Wedding anniversaries acknowledged on PhanaVision

228—Home runs, both teams

284—Hours spent mowing the field

420—Hot dogs launched by Phillie Phanatic

481—Longest home run (in feet) by Jason Grabowski, Los Angeles Dodgers, May 18

728—Phillies part-time gameday employees

4,795—Times "Happy Birthday" was sung by Phanstormers

10,500—Fans who participated in ballpark tours (in season)

12,117—Phillies foam fingers sold, the No. 1 retail item

23,939—Pitches thrown (12,063 by the opponents)

25,857—Phanatic dolls sold at Make Your Own Phanatic

44,710—Largest crowd, June 14 vs. Reds

59,890—Guests who played the Citizens Bank Games of Baseball

373,232—Promotional items given away at the gates

390,000—Group sales total

425,807—Online ticket sales (during the season)

803,000—Hot dogs sold

3,250,092—Club-record attendance

CHAPTER 5
MANAGERS

As a public relations person, you spend more time with the manager than anyone else. Seventeen different managers had to put up with me or vice versa. That includes interim managers. Until Charlie Manuel came along, I outlasted them all. As is the case with the rest of the world, managers come in all sizes and shapes, all kinds of personalities. Some tolerated the media; others didn't. When postgame media sessions grew in size and importance, some managers sought guidance. Others didn't. Some wanted a quick review of the game before meeting the media, some wanted stats, some wanted an idea of what questions might be forthcoming. Being in the press box during games, a PR person could get a read of the red flags.

Some were receptive to advice. I didn't have all the answers but learned from all those years in dealing with the media. I tried to make two points. One, don't fill dead air when doing interviews. Two, if you get asked a tough question, answer it as briefly as possible and repeat the same answer—no matter how many times the same question pops up. But sometimes the manager just wanted to vent after a loss, and those of us in PR were the listeners.

Gene Mauch

There was seldom a dull moment with Mauch. Phillies baseball had been dormant for a long time until the energetic and innovative 34-year-old manager arrived. He brought Phillies baseball back to life. I really enjoyed working with Mauch. He could be tough, yet charming—funny, yet grumpy. He could be a quote machine or an ice-making machine. If you tried to get close to him, he would ignore you. Ignore him, and he would slowly come around. Known as No. 4, the Little General, Little Napoleon, Skipper, Mauch was intensely into the game 24/7. Losses were followed by hours of reliving the pain.

Mauch demanded his players learn to play the game right. He preached executing fundamentals, situational hitting, getting runners in from third base with less than two outs, sacrifice bunts, squeeze bunts, hit-and-runs, etc. Mauch often bunted for a run early in the game. His theories: get one run, and the other team has to get two, and bunting for one run often leads to more.

"All of us, whether we want to admit it or not, learned from Gene and became better baseball people," explained Dallas Green, who pitched under Mauch. "[I] couldn't agree more," Tony Taylor said. "I learned how to play the game and win because of him."

Mauch always looked for an edge, oftentimes riding players on the other team. He felt if he could get into that player's head, it could affect the game and serve as an advantage for the Phillies. He moved the Phillies bullpen from left field to right at Connie Mack Stadium. There were two reasons. One, Mauch couldn't see into the left-field bullpen from the third-base dugout. There were rumors that relievers found a way underneath the stands to access food and beverages. Two, by relocating to right field, the bullpen coach could signal when balls were going to hit off the wall. So with the move, Mauch could see what his relievers were doing during the game, and coaches and players could get an edge.

Mauch loved to platoon, and I unknowingly got caught in the middle of one of his tirades on September 5, 1964. We were playing the San Francisco Giants at home. Alvin Dark was their manager, and he loved to try and out-maneuver Mauch. Bob Hendley, a left-hander, was scheduled to start for the Giants. I went over to their first-base dugout. Dark was sitting there. I copied his lineup, but there was a blank for the No. 9 hole where the pitcher normally bats. I looked at Dark and asked, "Is Hendley pitching?" He didn't say a word. Starters at Connie Mack Stadium warmed up near the dugouts, and Hendley was getting ready. I took that lineup to Mauch, and he started three right-handed bats, Cookie Rojas (center field), Alex Johnson (left field), and Gus Triandos (catcher) instead of Tony Gonzalez, Wes Covington, and Clay Dalrymple, respectively. The home team turns in its lineup first at home plate. When Mauch got Dark's lineup, Bob Bolin, a right-hander, who was throwing in the bullpen, was the starter and not Hendley. A right-handed pitcher is usually tougher for a right-handed hitter. I didn't think anything of it, especially when we scored four times in the first inning against Bolin en route to a 9–3 win. After the game, I received a tongue-lashing from Mauch. I don't know what would have happened if we had lost the game. Perhaps this book would end right here.

Earlier that season, we were playing a doubleheader in St. Louis, and I was on the trip. We lost the first game. During the second game, John Quinn called and said, "We just sold John Klippstein to the Twins. Go to the dugout and tell Gene not to use him in the game." Just as I get to the dugout, Mauch charges onto the field to argue with one of the umpires. When he argued, the veins in his neck stood out. Chris Short saw me in the dugout, "What are you doing here?" When I told him I needed to talk to Gene, Shorty said, "No you don't." Finally, Mauch returned to the dugout and he was still hot. Shorty went to the other end of the dugout and told Mauch I needed to see him, and the manager spun around and started toward me. "What do you want?" he barked. I gave him the message from Quinn. Gene didn't say a thing and returned to his end of the dugout. Shorty stood there laughing.

New York Mets catcher Jerry Grote reached into the Phillies third-base dugout at Connie Mack Stadium to catch a foul pop. Knowing an enemy player was fair game when he was reaching into the dugout, Mauch almost chopped off Grote's arms as he reached for the ball, and Grote did not catch it. Baseball rule No. 7.11 was changed that offseason. Now that would be considered interference, the ball would be considered dead, and the batter would be declared out.

Another time baseball was trying to speed up the game. Jim Bunning was pitching against the Mets at Shea Stadium and asked for a new baseball. Home-plate umpire Eddie Vargo refused. Mauch charged from the dugout, took the ball from Bunning, dropped it on the mound, stepped on it with his spikes, and flipped the damaged ball to Vargo. He did all this without saying one word.

Bill White was returning from his Achilles heel surgery in 1967. He could swing the bat but was limited in his mobility and running. We're playing the Mets—what was it with us and the Mets?—in Shea Stadium on April 21, and Mauch did the unorthodox again. He had White lead off and then replaced him after he grounded out to second base. In the bottom of the first, Bobby Wine went into the game at shortstop, Cookie Rojas, who was listed at short, went to second, and second baseman Taylor moved to first base.

Mauch was ejected by umpires quite often. One of the more unusual ones

---

occurred on May 1, 1968. While warming up between innings in New York, umpire Ed Vargo ruled that right-hander John Boozer violated the spitball rule by going to his mouth while on the mound. Mauch argued that the ruling was ridiculous because the umpire gave the batter a one-ball count before he even came to the plate. So Mauch ordered Boozer to do it again. Both were ejected.

Frank Lucchesi

Frank Lucchesi, known as "Skipper Lucchesi," was just what we needed when we were changing our image in 1970 in preparation for moving into the Vet. He spent 21 years in the minor leagues and was so thrilled at finally being in the major leagues. He was a PR person's dream come true as he was always willing to do interviews and appearances. Plus, the media loved him.

He was known for unusual antics in the minor leagues, once climbing a water tower beyond the outfield wall after he was ejected from the game. That obviously couldn't be done in the majors. He also was known to pile dirt on home plate following an ejection. He did that a couple of times in the big leagues. Skipper Lucchesi kept a yellow pad on his desk. After the game, he'd write down questions he thought the media would ask. He'd answer letters from nuns on his pregame radio show. Being Italian, Lucchesi was a perfect match in south Philadelphia and with mayor Frank Rizzo.

He deserves credit for Larry Bowa making it as a big leaguer. Bowa struggled mightily at the start of his rookie season in 1970, hitting .159 at the end of April. Lucchesi told Bowa he was going to stick with him no matter what. He refused to give up on him.

Lucchesi is in the record book for winning the last game at Connie Mack Stadium and the first at the Vet. We chatted one time about his Opening Day memories: "Well, I have two great memories and both were with the Phillies. 1970 at Connie Mack Stadium. After 21 years in the minor leagues, I was finally in the major leagues as a manager. Very emotional day for me. I was so happy. Then, 1971, the first game ever played in Veterans Stadium. Both hold very special places in my heart."

Danny Ozark

Born Daniel Leonard Orzechowski, he once attended a Dodgers tryout camp near his upstate New York home. One of the many other athletes there, trying to impress someone was named Paul Owens. Years later, Owens, as Phillies general manager, hired Danny Ozark to manage the Phillies. Ozark was not a media or fan favorite when hired, but he was perfect for this young team. He let the Phillies develop and play. He was considered a players manager and appeared to be easy going. But behind closed doors he would challenge players who were much younger. "Danny was the guy that took us from last to first," Bob Boone said. "He was the perfect manager for the Phillies in the '70s. He had the patience of Job and helped all of us grow up as men and players. He was a wonderful man."

He was genuinely a very nice person. Yes, he was known for some malapropisms, but Ozark knew baseball and he proved that. He also drank more coffee than anyone I've ever known. Ozark always seemed to have a cup in his hand before batting practice and after games.

He and Ginny had two children, a son (Dwain) and a daughter (Darlene), who was the same age as some of his players. Larry Christenson once asked Darlene for a date. According to Christenson, he was going to pick her up at their house when Ozark wasn't home. But when Christenson knocked on the door, Ozark answered. "LC, why the heck are you here?" he asked. Sheepishly, Christenson said, "I have a date with your daughter." Ozark hung his head, "Oh, no."

Ozark told me a great story about Tug McGraw. McGraw would stay in the clubhouse for the first couple of innings watching the game on TV, then come to the dugout for a couple of innings before going to the bullpen. "We all knew Tug could party. When he came to the dugout, I'd look at his shoe laces. If they were tied, he was ready to go. If they were untied, he'd had a long night," Ozark said laughing.

Ozark never got to a World Series with the Phillies. But in 2008 he came up from Vero Beach, Florida, on his own to root for the Phillies against the Tampa Bay Rays in the World Series. He'd often call to talk about that team. He'd come to Clearwater from Vero during spring training for a day, participating in a Major League Baseball Players Alumni Association charity event. Raised in the Dodgers organization, Ozark was a Phillie through and through. "Ginny and I really miss Philadelphia," Danny was quoted in a 2009 *Phillies Magazine* story published a month before he died. "We enjoyed our time there. That city is a great sports town. The fans are the greatest. They do express themselves, but that's okay. We made a lot of lifelong friends there."

Dallas Green

Dallas Green replaced Ozark and was his opposite. He wasn't afraid to publicly ruffle feathers. He'd bench anyone and play a rookie without hesitation. His manner led to clashes with some of our key players. "We not I" was his mantra. He had a booming voice and didn't mince his opinion. "I'm a screamer, yeller, and cusser," he said. "I never hold back." His nickname? Whispers. "I know, Baron, keep my mouth shut," he would say on many occasions. When the Phillies went to Houston for the playoffs in 1980, he ruffled the feathers of the wives by not allowing them on the charter flight.

Our relationship dates back to 1964. I didn't get to know him well during his playing days at the time. I remember one spring training when he was holding out for a bigger salary. Those unsigned were not allowed to work out with the team. I can still see him standing beyond a fence by first base at Jack Russell Stadium while his teammates were on the field.

Following his playing career, he moved into the front office as the director of player development and scouting. Owens took Green under his wing. At Owens' request, Green managed two years in rookie league ball in Huron, South Dakota, and Pulaski, Virginia. Two of his players at Huron were Greg Luzinski, a first baseman, and Manny Trillo. Both were just 17 years of age in their first pro seasons. Scouting and player development are the backbone of a successful baseball team. Under Owens we came up with some good young talent. With Green in charge, the trend continued.

After leading the Phillies to the 1980 World Championship, he later would leave to take charge of the Chicago Cubs, New York Yankees, and Mets. (He documents those experiences in the appropriately titled *The Mouth That*

Roared. I suggest you read it to get the full story and impact of this baseball lifer.) After being away from the Phillies for 17 years, he returned to his roots on April 23, 1998, as senior advisor to the general manager, Ed Wade. He's since served Pat Gillick and Ruben Amaro Jr. in the same role, attending all home games and spending time looking at the kids in the minor leagues. He has opinions and isn't afraid to share them.

Julie and I are privileged to call Dallas and his wife, Sylvia, among our closest friends. Has he mellowed? Has his voice grown softer? Front office employees are often approached loudly by Big D as he emphatically asks, "What have you done for the Phillies today?" Yeah, I'd say nothing has changed.

Jim Fregosi

Jim Fregosi had been around the game when he came to the Phillies. He could handle the media with charm or blistering responses. One time we were making a trade and I said to Fregosi, "Here are a couple of questions you might get asked." He slid his reading glasses to the edge of his nose, "Baron, I don't need your coaching." He was right. In spring training of 1996, Fregosi was giving me a hard time about something. "Jimmy, remember, I will outlast you," I told him. That fall, he was fired. As we left the press conference, he looked at me and said, "Baron, you were right."

While with the Phillies, though, he managed one of the wackiest teams, the 1993 National League champions. Once he left that bunch, he stopped smoking. In spring training of 2013, Mitch "Wild Thing" Williams came to Clearwater for the MLB Network. Fregosi was there that day scouting for the Atlanta Braves. I told him Williams was in the park, and Fregosi joked, "What's he trying to do? Get me to start smoking again?"

Fregosi's pitching coach was Johnny Podres, an old-school, cigarette-smoking baseball lifer. "Pods" somehow survived Williams' wild outings. But one time Tommy Greene was on the mound and struggling throwing strikes. Fregosi nodded to Podres to go to the mound and talk with Greene. "Jimmy's getting angry with me. Start throwing strikes and get him off my back," Podres told the young right-hander. Podres worked more on the mental approach than the mechanical one of a pitcher. He turned Curt Schilling from a thrower to a pitcher. When Podres died, Schilling attended the funeral in Glens Falls, New York, showing how much respect he had for Podres.

When Podres retired we brought him to spring training for a few years to observe and work with minor league pitchers. He loved to talk and had a ton of stories from his days with the Brooklyn Dodgers. One time I asked him, "With all the arm injuries pitchers have today, what was different during your days?" Without hesitation he said, "We drank more beer."

Fregosi, who passed away in 2014, was a longtime special assistant to the Atlanta Braves' GM. One of my most embarrassing winter meeting moments came at the huge Opryland Hotel in Nashville. GMs all had suites on the same floor of a certain wing. As I'm heading for Ed Wade's suite, I walked by an open door and saw Fregosi sitting there. For some reason, I mistakenly thought he was still our manager. So I walked right in and sat down to total silence. Fregosi, Bobby Cox, and John Schuerholz broke up laughing because I was in the Braves' suite. It took me a while to live that one down.

Terry Francona

Unlike Fregosi, Terry Francona had only managed in the minor leagues when we hired him. The night before his press conference, GM Lee Thomas had Francona and a bunch of us front office types to his Bucks County home to meet Francona for dinner. At one point it was suggested that Francona and I review the next day's press conference plans. We went into the kitchen and sat down at the table. I had thought of some questions he might face. After a couple of questions, I realized Francona didn't need much coaching. He was going to be fine. "Just be yourself tomorrow," I told him.

"That made me feel comfortable," Francona recalled. "Next day I get to the Vet, and we walk into the room for the press conference. Seeing all those people and cameras hit me like a ton of bricks. The lights were so bright it was hard to see. I was nervous big time. Whatever we talked about the night before was gone. I calmed a little when I saw Chet DiEmidio, a retired Philadelphia cop who once was an instructor in the White Sox system. He was the only friendly face I knew. I remember I tried to say, 'Being a manager isn't rocket science.' Instead it came out, 'It isn't dentistry.' I know I repeated myself many times on how excited I was to be the Phillies manager. Don Imus, the nationally syndicated radio talk show host, replayed my comments over and over. He buried me."

Francona survived the press conference, but his record with us wasn't very good. It wasn't him. We were just short of talent. He later proved how good he could be as a manager, winning two World Series with the Boston Red Sox.

Charlie Manuel

When Wade made a tough decision to let Bowa go as manager, he hired Charlie Manuel. Media and fans got on Manuel initially, ridiculing the man. Critics claimed he didn't know how to manage. To them he was "Good old Charlie," a guy with an accent who stumbled over words and got mixed up with his comments.

Slowly, everyone began to realize Manuel knew baseball. Heck, it's been his entire life. Was he easy going? Yes. Would he unload on a player behind closed doors? Yes. He may be ticked off inside, but he never showed it. He can laugh and he can get mad, really mad. One of his sayings is "know thyself." We can all be better if we "know thyself."

As the leader he didn't panic and he was always positive, which is damn tough over a 162-game season. He was the same way everyday through peaks and valleys, ups and downs, highlights and lowlights. Oh, he could be grumpy one day, but we are all like that from time to time. He loved baseball, loved to tell stories, and loved to talk hitting. Manuel is a terrific banquet speaker, too. He has a story that brings down the house every time. "Growing up, I was one of 11 children," Manuel said. "I never slept alone until I got married." Matter of fact, I've used that story many, many times during speaking engagements. It gets a big laugh every time.

To me, Manuel and Ozark had similarities. Both weren't popular hires, both were considered players managers, both were loyal to their players, both didn't criticize players publically, both could air out players behind closed doors, both won division championships, and both had long tenures that ended during disappointing seasons. There, however, is a difference. Ozark won three straight division titles but couldn't get the club to the next level, the World Series. It will be a long, long time before someone puts up better numbers and more championships than Manuel did with the Phillies. Hey, the only Philadelphia baseball manager to win more games than Manuel was Connie Mack, who managed the Philadelphia A's for 50 years.

It has been my experience that once a manager is around for six or more seasons, their methods, their voices no longer seem to matter. It isn't the fault of the manager or the players, it just happens. Mauch, Ozark, and Fregosi went through the same thing with the Phillies. Then Manuel joined the list of ex-Phillies managers. High expectations with a veteran team went down the tubes after the All-Star Game in 2013.

Fans and media complained that Manuel didn't receive the respect he deserved. He should have been allowed to finish the season. Seldom is there an ideal time to change managers or an easy way to do it. Ruben Amaro Jr. had made up his mind. It would have been worse to let Manuel finish the season, knowing he wouldn't be back in 2014. Some day, he will be honored by the Phillies, and fans will get to express their appreciation for a person who attained the status of a legend. We were privileged to be around this humble man for eight-plus seasons. Manuel took us to places we'd never been. Thanks for the ride, Charlie.

CHAPTER 6
GENERAL MANAGERS

John Quinn

Once I joined the Phillies, general managers were also privileged to my trade ideas. But none of my brilliant suggestions made it. In reality my job was to announce the deals—not make them. I once suggested we trade for a certain pitcher. Mr. Quinn replied, "He's nothing but a .500 pitcher." I thought to myself, *Geez, we're playing .400 ball now. Let's get to .500.*

Mr. Quinn was a gentleman from the old school with a starched, white-collar shirt, cuff links, suit, tie, and polished shoes. I never saw him without a tie, and I never, ever saw him without his suit coat or sport coat. First time I met Mr. Quinn—I always referred to him that way—was in his office after I had joined the Phillies. The meeting was quick. "Son, you can learn a lot in this business if you keep your mouth shut and your ears open," he said. I also received some other advice from him. "If you want to be in the game, you have to learn to sleep fast," he said. I always remembered that because it popped up from time to time with day games following late night games. When talking trades, Mr. Quinn, the manager, and farm director were involved. Every now and then, I was allowed in as a spectator. Several times someone would mention expanding a deal. His response: "Don't muddy the waters."

Mr. Quinn had been the GM of the Boston Braves and then the Milwaukee Braves when the team moved to Wisconsin, where they had tremendous success, winning two pennants and the 1957 World Series. All that success filled County Stadium. He often talked about how much fun it used to be. I thought, *gee, I'm having fun.* Decades later, the game wasn't as much fun for me as it had been. I remembered what he had said.

A baseball lifer, he had a reputation of being a difficult negotiator when it came to player contracts. There were no agents during his time—just the GM and the player, head-to-head, year-by-year. Mr. Quinn joined the Phillies the offseason after Richie Ashburn won the 1958 batting title by hitting .350. Ashburn went in to negotiate his contract. He was offered a $1,000 raise. "He told me I hit too many singles," Ashburn said. "I said, 'If I hit them any harder, they would be outs.'"

Mr. Quinn helped me grow as a person and in my position. In one of our many conversations, I mentioned that it was fate that I wound up with the

Phillies. He said, "No, it was faith." Early on, I was told when we would make an announcement and had no advance idea what was happening. As time went by, I was given advance notice and asked for an opinion as to how and when we would make an announcement. Obviously, I had gained the respect and trust of Mr. Quinn.

I remember being called to Bob Carpenter's estate in Wilmington, Delaware, on a Saturday morning in 1972, June 3. He let me know Paul Owens would be replacing Mr. Quinn as GM, following the afternoon game. Mr. Carpenter asked that only the writers covering the game be there and that there be no press conference. I understood, but a new GM is a big story. I debated what to do. What about the columnists and electronic media? Finally, I called the three TV sports directors and confidentially asked that they send a crew to the game, no questions asked. I didn't want to disrespect Mr. Carpenter but felt it was the right thing to do. In the top of the ninth inning, Chris Wheeler and I escorted the media to Mr. Carpenter's office. There was a lot of grumbling because the game hadn't ended. Mr. Carpenter told the media group that Quinn was retiring and being replaced by Owens.

Mr. Quinn's first trade with the Phillies was sending veteran third baseman Gene Freese to the Chicago White Sox for a promising young outfielder, Johnny Callison. His last trade was a Hall of Fame deal, getting Steve Carlton for Rick Wise.

Paul Owens

I followed the Phillies closely as a kid, including their minor leagues. In 1956 the Olean, New York, club in the Pennsylvania, Ontario, and New York League produced a batting champion who hit .368. It happened again the next year when he hit .407. That 33-year-old player—not exactly a young prospect— was named Paul Owens. After World War II, he returned to his Salamanca, New York, roots and transferred from Rider College to St. Bonaventure. He was headed for a teaching career when the Olean team invited him to try out in 1951. He was looking at it as a summer job while on a teaching break.

He paid 75 cents to get into the park. The general manager said it wasn't a tryout—rather they needed him on the field. He got a couple of hits the first game and signed a contract for $175 per month. Four years later the Phillies purchased the Olean club, which had been an independent team, and Owens was a player-manager for the 1956–57 seasons. Gene Martin, then the Phillies director of minor league clubs, moved Owens to Bakersfield, California, to manage that team in 1958 and 1959. Martin then convinced him to become a scout, giving him the entire Southwest. Considering himself a "field person," Owens reluctantly changed his career path to scouting.

In 1964 he was the coordinator of the Phillies spring training camp for Class A players in Leesburg, Florida. Ruly Carpenter was assigned to the camp to get educated on the process. In 1965 Owens was brought to Philadelphia to oversee player development and scouting. While he worked with Carpenter, changes were made in the 20-man scouting staff. Many longtime scouts were let go, and new blood was brought in. "We weren't signing big league players. I hired some new people, and we signed some guys who made it through the first [1965] draft," he said. "That year alone we got Larry Bowa and Denny Doyle for little money each."

During his tenure of heading player development and scouting, he convinced Carpenter that a training complex was needed in Clearwater. The four-diamond Carpenter Complex opened in 1967 and housed all the Phillies minor league players. The previous year Triple A and Double A clubs were in Dade City, Florida, and the Single A players were in Leesburg, Florida, with Owens. Neither was near Clearwater where the big club trained. He also started a Florida Fall Instruction League program at the complex. Centralized, consistent instruction and player evaluation was now possible.

In 1969 the Phillies received the Topps Award for the best minor league program, a program that produced Bowa, Doyle, Greg Luzinski, Bob Boone, and Mike Schmidt. Owens' career changed again when he became general manager. A little more than a month later, he replaced his friend, Frank Lucchesi, as manager. His mission: to find out who could play and who couldn't. If they couldn't play, they would be gone. At age 59 he returned to the dugout in the middle of the 1983 season and led the Phillies to the National League pennant. His reign as GM was unmatched in team history,

Paul Owens, the team's legendary general manager, and Tug McGraw were honored during a video tribute prior to the opening game at Citizens Bank Park.

climaxing with the franchise's first World Series championship in 1980. It can be said that he single-handedly turned the Phillies franchise around and may well be the best "baseball" man in club history.

Nicknamed "the Pope" for his resemblance to Pope Paul VI, Owens was a man of enormous patience. When talking trade he'd outwait the other guy. Owens had a clock that seemingly used all 24 hours particularly at the winter meetings. Being in his suite at 1 or 2 AM would be something all of us would eventually experience as a normal time of the day. I don't know how he did it. "You gotta have bounceability," he would say. While he was bouncing, the rest of us were dragging.

He was the best judge of people I've ever met—not just players. He could tell you everything about another employee or a player but his or her name. One tiny example: Mac Scarce was a lefty rookie reliever in 1972. He pitched well in a spring training game in Lakeland, Florida. After the game Pope and I were walking toward the clubhouse, and here comes Scarce. I thought to myself, *This is going to be interesting. What is he going to call him?* Pope nodded and said, "Nice going…*big lefty.*"

The Pope loved grass roots baseball, scouting, and developing. Buddy Harris was an outstanding pitcher at Roxborough High School in 1966. He was going to scout Harris personally and asked me to go with him. Unlike most scouts Owens didn't like to sit behind home plate. "Too much chit-chatting among the scouts," he said. "Then after the game, they compare radar reports." Instead he watched the game down the right-field foul line. He wanted to see Harris throw from a different angle, wanted to see him in the third-base dugout especially after a rough inning or an inning in which a teammate committed an error. How did the kid handle adversity?

As the GM he traveled most of the time with the Phillies. That way he felt he could get to know his players better. He'd get to the ballpark early and sit in the stands, observing both teams' batting practice. Owens made mental notes of players who worked hard or loafed in going through the motions. He remembered seeing Richie Hebner of the Pittsburgh Pirates busting it during batting practice—both in the cage and in the field. When the Phillies needed a first baseman in 1977, Owens signed Hebner as a free agent. He had a rare sense to see not only the physical tools of a player, but also what was inside the player. He sought the kind of people that you would want in your foxhole when you went to battle, which was appropriate, considering his own period of service for the country.

Owens also could air out people with the best of them. I've seen and heard him verbally blast players, writers, and fans. Add me to that list. We were on the last night of a 10-stop, week-long caravan in Trenton, New Jersey. He looked tired and had taken in a few drinks. I was concerned that he would embarrass himself, so I said, "Pope, to shorten the program tonight, it would be okay if you didn't speak." He glared at me. "I'll talk to you later," he said.

Owens stood up and delivered one of the most heartwarming speeches I've ever heard. He didn't have a note in front of him but went on about all the well-mannered children that were there, congratulated the parents for raising such impressive kids, stressed the importance of family and how families have made America such a great country. The audience was mesmerized. After the banquet I waited by the bus. I knew my medicine was coming and I wanted to take it as quickly as possible—like how I dealt with that yucky stuff Mom would make me take. He approached and started poking me in the chest with his right forefinger. "Who do you think you are, telling me when I can speak and when I can't? I know what I'm doing. Don't you ever do that again." I didn't, believe me.

On another caravan Owens decided to stay out with the players when we got back to the Vet. He didn't get home until 2 AM. Marcelle, his wife, was waiting for him. Pope made me out to be the bad guy, and I took the fall. "Larry Shenk keeps us out all night," he said. "That's the last time I'm going on the caravan." Marcelle turned around and went back to bed.

At the expansion meeting in Montreal in 1968, we were having dinner in the hotel restaurant, which wasn't crowded. Some guy under the influence kept coming over to Owens. "I know you, I really do, pal." One time he patted Owens on the back, but it was a hard pat. Owens stood up, grabbed the guy by his suit coat, and tossed him into an empty nearby table. Dishes, glasses, forks, and knives were flying everywhere. The guy was flat on his back with his feet sticking up above the broken table. Owens barked, "I've had enough, understand?"

There were times when you'd think Owens didn't know what was going on with the team. But he didn't miss a thing. One time during a press conference, he was asked a question, but he never answered it. Afterward I said, "Pope, you never answered that question about Dick Allen." He smiled and said, "Every now and then, you have to dance a little soft-shoe shuffle."

While he was tough, there was a huge soft spot in his heart. When we traded Willie Montanez to the San Francisco Giants for Garry Maddox in 1975, he called Montanez to his office. When told he was traded, Montanez began to cry. I walked in moments later, and both Montanez and Owens were crying. He cried when he, Dallas Green, and Tug McGraw received the World Series trophy.

The Pope was among the first GMs to give contracts longer than a year. Bowa went to Owens' office to negotiate a contract. Owens loved to tell the story: "Larry was always hyper and he started talking about needing a raise. I was playing with a yo-yo…up and down, up and down, and Bo was getting more and more jittery. I was having fun with the yo-yo and I finally said, 'I can't give you that much of a raise, but I tell you what I will do. I'll give you a two-year contract.'" Bowa was so excited he came into the PR office to tell us about his new contract.

When Green was in charge of player development and scouting, Owens and Ruly Carpenter were always conversing on player issues. Most of the time they agreed. But when Owens traded Tommy Underwood and Rick Bosetti to the St. Louis Cardinals for Bake McBride at the June 15 trade deadline in 1977, sparks flew. Ruly Carpenter and Green were not happy to give up a young arm like Underwood for an older outfielder. The trade deadline then was midnight. The deal was agreed upon just minutes before the deadline, but there was an issue. Carpenter was concerned about the health of McBride's knees. It took hours for the Cardinals doctor (Stan London) and Phillies team physician (Philip Marone) to connect and review the medical reports. Once those reports were cleared, the deal was final, and McBride turned out to be a big part of the world championship three years later.

Owens loved his own family but also loved another family, the Phillies. He had a special way of making everyone feel part of that family whether it was an All-Star player or a summer intern. If he didn't know your name, he simply said, "Hey, big guy." He had the ability to make everyone feel like a longtime friend. He genuinely loved people and made them feel special. Many a night it would take him 30 minutes to go from his parking spot to the Phillies offices because, as he described it, "I was chit-chatting with the fans."

There were times when he couldn't always explain his decisions. He'd just say, "Sometimes you fly by the seat of your pants." Owens could offer sound advice. He could make us laugh with his humor and malapropisms. "If you don't change, you'll be left behind," he said. "When you hire someone, you should hire a person who was good enough to take your job." He also had a good sense of humor. While riding a bus through the Pocono mountains on another Phillies caravan, the bus was creeping up this long hill. From the back of the bus, he yelled: "Hey bussie. You're going so slow a turtle is passing us." Other memorable lines included: "You can lead a horse to water, but you can't stick his damn face in it" and "You can't change the spots on a zebra." While riding in a cab, he said to the driver, "The music is a little loud. Can you turn it down 12 disciples?"

When planning for the Vet's closing ceremonies, Ed Wade said he would bring Pope, whose health was failing. We didn't know until late that day if he would make it. Everyone, including players and fans alike, was touched that he was there. The ovation that Owens received was one of the many highlights that afternoon. He got to step on home plate one last time and was part of the victory lap after the ceremonies, sharing a golf cart ride with Wade and Green while the large group of players walked. Wade said it best: "Without the Pope, there wouldn't have been anything to commemorate."

Owens died on December 26, 2003, three months after the closing ceremonies. When I got the call from Wade that Owens had died, I went to the office around 4 PM to write the obituary and notify the media. More than four hours later, I finished. I was the only person in the Vet offices. It was quiet. Except for lights in the PR office and hallways, there was total darkness. It was eerie because the Vet was empty in more ways than one. In preparation for implosion, there were no more blue seats and no green turf. Now, there was no Paul Owens, whose office had been right around the corner from mine for so many years.

Then, a smile came to my face. On October 21, 1980, at 11:29 PM, the Phillies won their first World Series. The Vet and the Delaware Valley erupted with joy. Veterans Stadium will forever be remembered as the home of the world champion Phillies, a team built by Owens. It is his legacy. His legacy has also been documented in Clearwater, where his vision of a training complex became a reality in 1967. In February 2012 a memorial bust of Owens was dedicated at Carpenter Complex, a permanent remembrance of his legacy in Clearwater. Two years prior the clubhouse was renovated, and a second floor was added. At that time the clubhouse was officially named the "Paul Owens Training Facility." The Carpenter Complex, the Paul Owens Training Facility, and Bright House Field give the Phillies the best spring training facilities in Florida.

Lee Thomas

He went from player development with the St. Louis Cardinals to our GM in 1988. Like the Pope he had experience in every phase of the game. He'd even been the traveling secretary for the Cardinals. Thomas is a pleasant person with an easy smile but also a fuse that can be short. I guess that's why he was called "Mad Dog."

He kept the public relations department busy because he made a lot of player moves. In the space of 16 days of June in the 1989 season, three trades brought John Kruk, Randy Ready, Lenny Dykstra, Terry Mulholland, Roger McDowell, and Charlie Hayes to us. The foundation of a solid team was taking form. Mitch Williams (1991) and Curt Schilling (1992) were acquired in trades at the end of spring training. That season he made a change in the dugout, bringing in his former teammate with the California Angels, Jim Fregosi, as manager. With all the changes, last place was the end result.

But that winter the roster kept changing. Danny Jackson, David West, Larry Andersen, Milt Thompson, Pete Incaviglia, and Jim Eisenreich were obtained. We were hot after free agent pitcher David Cone at the winter meetings in 1992. Thomas also had a meeting with Dennis Gilbert, Inky's agent, at the same time he was going after Cone. Thomas looked at me. "Baron, when Dennis gets here, take him into the next room and entertain him for a few minutes." I had never met Gilbert and didn't know what to say or do. I tried some small talk until Thomas reappeared.

Thomas had put together a club of rejects that could play ball. Ninety-seven wins replaced 92 losses. The Phillies surprised the world by getting to Game 6 of the World Series in 1993. Of the 25 players on that postseason roster, only Darren Daulton, Mickey Morandini, Kevin Stocker, and Kim Batiste were homegrown. Thomas acquired all 10 pitchers, an unheard of figure. He earned the Major League Executive of the Year award from *The Sporting News*. The only other Phillies executive to win that award was owner Bob Carpenter in 1949. In Thomas' final year in 1997, he acquired Bobby Abreu, an expansion draft day acquisition, from the Tampa Bay Devil Rays for Stocker. Abreu starred for the Phillies for nine seasons.

Ed Wade

A graduate of Temple University with a journalism degree, Wade was working at the *Williamsport Gazette* newspaper when he contacted me

Following the 2000 season, general manager Ed Wade looks on as the team names Larry Bowa manager in a press conference at Loews Hotel.

looking for a job in baseball. We brought him aboard as the intern for the PR department for the 1977 season. Wade laughs when remembering his compensation: "$2.50 an hour and all the Tastykakes I could eat. Add $12 a game for typing the play-by-play. I was also given time to visit with usherettes pregame, which led to meeting my future wife." His "office" was the copy room right around the corner from the PR offices. He soon got a degree in copying and seemed to know more about the Xerox copier than the company's service person. Following his internship his journey took him to Houston (assistant PR director), Pittsburgh (PR director), and Tal Smith Enterprises, where he learned the contract business side of baseball. He returned to us in 1989 as an assistant to Thomas. Nine years later he replaced Thomas.

In his first spring training that year, my wife, Julie, was in the PR office at Jack Russell Stadium after a game. Wade walked by, "Baron, can I see you a minute?" I followed him to his office and then returned to the PR office. Julie said, "I guess he's really your boss." With his journalism background, there were times when he'd write his own press release and e-mail it to me.

As with any GM, Wade made some deals that worked and some that didn't. Eventually, he was replaced. He deserves credit for bringing Bowa back to the Phillies as manager, then removing him and hiring Charlie Manuel. Both were tough, tough decisions. The homegrown core of the 2008 World Champions were brought into the Phillies on his clock. Pat Gillick acknowledged Wade after we won it all that fall.

Ruben Amaro Jr.

When he took over as GM, I thought, *Geez, I remember when he was born! And now he's our GM.* I became friends with his mom and dad, watched Junior grow up, and remember him as a bat boy in the 1980 World Series. I wrote a press release that we had traded for him and then another press release that we traded him. With both Wade and Amaro, life came full circle for me.

CHAPTER 7
SCOUTS

Spending hours following kids and projecting how they will perform when they become men, scouts are the backbone of any successful big league club. Scouting is certainly not a precise science. For months the scouts live in a car, traveling to endless hotels as they check and re-check prospects from their territory. They sit through rain delays, scorching sun, and—sometimes— long and boring ballgames. Stopwatches, radar guns, scorebooks, and sun- screen are their tools. Some sit among the pack behind home plate, reading radar numbers. Others will choose more private spots, looking for a different angle. Laptops provide their source for filing reports back to the home office. Are they unheralded? Without a doubt.

Once the scouts have done their digging, young prospects are turned over to the player development department, another unsung department. Managers, coaches, instructors, and athletic trainers all put in long hours polishing play- ers. Scouts get to know a player's mother and father. Managers and coaches oftentimes become fathers away from home, especially to high schoolers who are not living with mom and dad for the first time. It is a big adjustment. They were big fish in a small pond, but in pro ball they become little fish in a big pond. Before the draft came along in 1965, scouts were also expected to be salesmen. In addition to judging talent and heart, they needed to get to know the prospect, his parents, friends, and girlfriend. They were competing with every other baseball club.

The scouting of Curt Simmons is a great example of how the scouting process used to work. Simmons grew up in a small town, Egypt, north of Allentown, Pennsylvania. A hard-throwing left-handed pitcher, he was on every team's radar out of high school. "The scouts used to sit on the front porch because they didn't want to miss a thing," Simmons said. "I remember Mom got so annoyed that she chased them off the porch. Cy Morgan was the Phillies scout. Dad finally told him, 'Why don't you bring your team here to play our team?'" Cy carried the message back to the Phillies offices.

Because the Phillies were idle on Monday, June 2, 1947, owner Bob Carpenter sent the team to Egypt Park for an exhibition game against the squad with Simmons, who would pitch for the town team that competed in the Twilight League. (Somehow, I don't imagine that happening these days.)

The day before, the Phillies lost to the Chicago Cubs 4–3 at Shibe Park. Facing Simmons the Phillies wound up in a 4–4, nine-inning tie, a game, which was called by darkness. Except for shortstop, the Phillies fielded the same starting lineup that faced the Cubs. Simmons held the Phillies to seven hits, walked three, and struck out 11. An error led to an eighth-inning, game-tying run that kept the Phillies from losing.

The next day the Detroit Tigers and Boston Red Sox scouts offered a $58,000 signing bonus to Simmons. "That was a lot of money," Simmons said. "But Dad had told the Phillies they would have the last crack." Morgan offered $60,000 plus a promise the Phillies would call him up in September and give him an additional $5,000. It was the biggest signing bonus in baseball. Morgan's salesmanship paid off.

During his senior year in high school in 1957, Bobby Wine was a much sought-after shortstop. "Dale Jones was the Phillies scout and he started following me my junior year," Wine said. "He became like a father figure to me. After graduation we went to Philadelphia on the train, met [Phillies owner] Mr. Carpenter, and I signed, got $4,000. When I got home, the Yankees, Reds, and Red Sox came calling, but I said, 'Sorry, I signed with the Phillies.'"

Once the draft came along, salesmanship became less important. You could only sign the players you drafted. Getting to know the prospect and his family was valuable but to a lesser degree. Signability became the key inside information the scouts would need to find out. That first draft took place in the Commodore Hotel in New York City. Each team was assigned to a round table. Paul Owens conducted the draft for us. There was a lot of buzzing going on that day. Teams were selecting players of whom other teams didn't have scouting reports, and everyone seemed to be kind of nervous.

Scouting the physical tools of a prospect is the easy part of the job. But you also have to find out what's inside a kid, what's in his head, and what's in his heart. We have area scouts assigned to a certain territory. The boss of these people for the Phillies is Marti Wolever, assistant general manager of amateur scouting. When an area scout has a hot prospect, many of the others will also see that player, including on occasion Ruben Amaro, Pat Gillick, Dallas Green, and Benny Looper. We also have a staff that scouts outside of the United States. Sal Agostinelli is our director of international scouting. He oversees Venezuela, the Dominican Republic, Mexico, and Panama. In addition there are numerous independent contractor scouts also known as "bird dogs." They aren't full-time but act as scouts under area scouts. We also have a presence in Australia, Netherlands, Aruba, Colombia, Italy, South Africa, Japan, Korea, and Canada.

Wolever and his staff of coordinators and supervisors usually convene at Citizens Bank Park for 10 to 12 days before the draft. The war room is set up on the Hall of Fame Club level of the baseball administration offices. Magnetic boards surround the room. Eligible players on both the college and high school level are then ranked by position. Laptops have replaced bulky three-ring notebooks that used to contain pages and pages of written reports. Cell phones have replaced landlines. Area scouts are called constantly for updates during the ranking process, which can include heated debates.

We've obtained a lot of quality players through the draft over the years. There also have been some duds, something that happens to all clubs and all sports. We had a run, starting in 1996 that produced some amazing talent: Jimmy Rollins (1996), Pat Burrell (1998), Chase Utley (2000), Ryan Howard (2001), and Cole Hamels (2002). During that time frame, we also signed Carlos Ruiz as an amateur free agent (1998).

Bob Poole followed Rollins and filed the following after seeing him play two games (14 innings) in March of 1996: "This youngster can pick and throw. He has range, quickness, supple hands, strong/accurate arm. Excellent instincts and field smarts. Switch hitter; swing is compact with short stride, makes sharp contact from both sides. Tool-wise, it's all there, except power, but it comes in a small package. Will be an early pick by a club that will go for tools over size. He CAN play and he can play shortstop in the major leagues."

Burrell was a power-hitting third baseman at the University of Miami, a long way from his northern California roots. Here is Miguel Machado's report of him from April 1998: "An impressive and attractive young athlete with a very good approach at the plate. Stays back and keeps shoulders in at the moment of hitting; abundant and impressive raw power with remarkable bat speed. It's not very often that we find selective power hitters, and he is one of

Is that really Ryan Howard wearing No. 12? Yes, that was his number when he made his big league debut on September 1, 2004, and again in spring training of 2005.

the select group. I believe very strongly in his offensive tools. He is hard-working with excellent determination and confidence to play in the big leagues."

Allan Lewis was a base-stealing outfielder from Panama who spent parts of six seasons in the majors and another seven in the minors. He gets the credit for finding Ruiz. His December 1998 report: "Good athlete and good ability. Does his job in a very quiet way. Should develop into a good hitter. Should improve with games under his belt. Has all the basics you look for but needs a lot of work. Outstanding kid and a hard worker."

Utley was originally drafted by the Los Angeles Dodgers in the second round in 1997, but he opted to attend his hometown school, UCLA, instead. Numerous Phillies scouts followed him in college ball. When he became a junior and eligible to be drafted, we selected him in the first round (15th overall) in 2000.

A scout, Paul Scott, saw Utley play three games and filed the following on May 31, 2000, just before the draft: "Live, athletic body. Long arms, small waist. Quiet, but aggressive. Quick bat. Sneaky power. Good, soft hands. Good instincts and good base runner. Active, moves around a lot. Can drive the ball the other way. Hitch in swing, but hands and bat are in good position at trigger. He will be a starting second baseman on a pennant winner. Top of the order hitter. Should move through the system quickly."

Garrett Atkins, who was drafted by the Colorado Rockies in the fifth round, played third, and Utley played second for the Bruins. "My best friend at UCLA was Garrett Atkins," Utley said. "We were following the draft on the computer. Just as my name came up on the screen, I got a call from Mike Arbuckle and Ed Wade welcoming me to the Phillies. I'll never forget that moment."

Wolever had seen Howard in two games in 2001 at Southwest Missouri State University, the year he was eligible for the draft. His May 29 report: "Large-framed, huge-bodied athlete, similar to Willie Mays Aikens. Low fastball hitter with above average power from pole to pole. Above average bat speed. Average to slightly above average hands at first base. May have best raw power of 2001 draft. Better as a sophomore and USA last summer. Would gamble on power."

A couple other scouts also felt he was better as a sophomore. Perhaps because of the multiple scouts following him, he developed a case of "draftitis" and put extra pressure on himself as an upperclassman. When it came time for the draft, the Phillies picked him in the fifth round, selecting him 140th over-all. Many went before him, including Joe Mauer, David Wright, and Mark Teixeira. Few matched his production. Howard had the best power of anyone in the draft and carried it into the minor leagues and then the majors.

Hamels was an outstanding high school pitching prospect in San Diego. Arbuckle was the last Phillies scout to see him before the 2002 draft and wrote: "Excellent pitchability, command, and presence for a high school pitcher. Around the plate with everything and has good feel for pitching. Competes and challenges well. Uses change-up very well and has good motion on it with good sink. Curve is average at times with some bite. Will move quickly [in pro ball] for a high school kid. Has good ceiling as a potential [No.] 1 or 2 starter. A definite consideration at the 17th selection."

Scouts are not limited to amateurs. Teams have scouts who concentrate on professional players of all levels. Some are assigned only to major league clubs. The GM may be working on a deal and will send his major league scout to fol-low a certain team or player. Once again, looking at the skills isn't the biggest item. That major league scout will spend time picking up inside information from writers and broadcasters as well as watching games. You have to gather as much intelligence as possible.

One of the best known pro scouts was Hugh Alexander. Known as "Poor Old Hughie" or "Uncle Hughie," he spent 64 years over eight decades as a scout, including a long stint with the Phillies. "He's my eyes and ears," Owens once said of Hughie, who might have been the best storyteller ever in baseball. "Hughie, you keep telling the same stories. Why don't you number them, let us know the number, and we'll laugh?" Owens kidded him.

Alexander excelled at getting information on players. He was loved and respected by all in the game and had multiple sources to tap. He certainly wasn't an introvert. The media also loved him. He walked into the press din-ing room at the Vet one time and said, "I've got 11 trades in my pocket right now we could make. That's right, *11*." Writers tripped over each other, trying to get to Alexander for a scoop, though I don't believe we made any of those 11 trades.

He had opinions and wasn't bashful. We were fighting for the pennant in 1983 and looking for a right-handed bat to add to the roster before September 1. (Players acquired after that date aren't eligible for the postseason.) Owens and Alexander targeted Sixto Lezcano of the San Diego Padres, who were looking for pitching prospects. One was Lance McCullers, a right-hander. We were reluctant to give up McCullers, but Alexander spoke up: "Never let a Class A pitcher stop you from making a deal. Too much can happen. He can get hurt, level out, or go backward." McCullers was one of four pitchers traded for Lezcano, joining Darren Burroughs, Marty Decker, and Ed Wojna. With Lezcano on the club, we got to the World Series while none of the four pitchers became impact players in the majors.

CHAPTER 8
BECOMING A
BASEBALL MAN

Growing up in Myerstown, a small town in Lebanon County in Central Pennsylvania, the baseball bug bit me. I'm not sure about a specific date, time, or event, but watching the Phillies in the 1950 World Series on a small, black and white Motorola television does provide some vague memories. WLBR-AM (Lebanon) carried Phillies games, and I became a die-hard fan. I rarely missed a game on radio with Gene Kelly, By Saam, and Claude Haring. To this day I still prefer radio vs. TV because it allows you to imagine *There's a deep fly ball to left.*

My resume featured Little League, American Legion, and high school baseball. I knew how to play, but I didn't have the skills. While in college one summer, though, I was the groundskeeper of the Myerstown Legion field. If I couldn't play well on the grass, I could at least mow it. Every town had a baseball team. We were the Myerstown Patriots. As a youngster, I was the bat boy for home games and trips to nearby towns. Eventually, I moved up to a bench player. I looked good in a uniform and on the bench. I also invented my own baseball game using dice for a full 154-game season. I kept stats, and the Phillies lost very few games. Mom used to say, "I wish you'd spend as much time with your studies."

At one point WLBR stopped carrying Phillies games. The only place I could faintly hear games was on WIP-AM out of Philadelphia. Atlantic Richfield Refining Company was a major sponsor of Phillies broadcasts. For a few years, they conducted a junior Phillies broadcasters contest. I sent my letter (1957), and lo and behold, WIP called to say I was their finalist.

Mom, Dad, and I made a trip to Philadelphia for a pregame dinner with Kelly, Saam, and Haring at the Drake Hotel before going to Shibe Park. Eight contestants taped one inning. One would be selected to broadcast one inning live later in the season. My Pennsylvania Dutch accent didn't help nor did my blown call of a fly ball that turned out to be a mere pop-up in the infield. But sitting in the press box pretending to broadcast a Phillies game was such a thrill. I also once auditioned at WLBR for an on-air job doing news updates on weekends. Given news copy to read, I completely butchered foreign dignitary names. I guess a career in broadcasting wasn't going to happen.

You also could follow the Phillies in the newspaper. The *Lebanon Daily*

As one of eight finalists in the Atlantic Richfield Junior Sportscasters Contest in 1957, I received the chance to tape an inning of a Phillies game from the Connie Mack Stadium press box. The winner got to broadcast one inning live later in the season. I didn't win.

News had a small sports section and didn't always carry a lot about the games. Jack and Grace Bicher lived a couple of blocks away on Main Street. They had home delivery of *The Philadelphia Inquirer*. During one summer I'd often bike to their house, sit on the porch, and read their paper before they did.

Graduation from Myerstown High School came in 1956. My favorite teacher, George (Rinso) Marquette, taught geography. He had played three years of pro ball in the minors. I'd go to school early to talk baseball. In 1957 I decided to go to college to become an elementary teacher. Mom was a teacher at one time. Dad worked in a steel mill and once said, "I don't care what you want to do, but you're not working in the mill." I applied to Kutztown and Millersville State Colleges. I was rejected at Kutztown but accepted at Millersville in 1957, which turned out to be a blessing.

At MSC I became the statistician for the football and basketball teams but not baseball for some reason. As a basketball manager, one of the jobs was to call the Lancaster newspapers with game information, which I loved doing. Earl Hite was an English professor and the advisor to the college's newspaper, *The Snapper*. He encouraged me to join the staff and write sports. Mr. Hite became my mentor. He was a big baseball fan. His team was the Pittsburgh Pirates, so we had a lot to talk about. The sports editor one year was Phil Itzoe from York, Pennsylvania. He was a Baltimore Orioles fan, and I was a Phillies fan. We became good friends. Little did anyone know that our paths would cross in the major leagues some day.

As an elementary education major, I was interested but not as dedicated as my classmates. That's because I still had Phillies blood in me. You'll be happy to know my initial audiovisual presentation was about the Phillies minor league system. Hey, kids in grade school need to know and understand the minor league system.

The greatest thing at MSC was meeting Julie Hollingsworth, a tall blonde from Kennett Square, Pennsylvania. She was a year behind me and also an elementary education major and—very importantly—she was a Phillies fan. She even knew their catcher was Clay Dalrymple! A degree in elementary education was attained in 1961, but more importantly, I met my wife-to-be at dear old MSC. A true blessing. I wanted to succeed in life because of her.

With my MSC diploma in hand, I headed back home but went through Lebanon and stopped by the *Daily News*. I needed a summer job until I landed a teaching position and was told about a full-time position as general reporter that included writing sports on Friday nights. I took the job. If it didn't work out, I could pursue teaching.

Following the Phillies 1961 season, a change was made in the Phillies publicity position. I applied and was rejected. After the 1962 season was over, another change was made. I applied again, this time on *Daily News* letterhead for that position or any position. General manager John Quinn replied: "After reviewing many applicants, we have selected Charles Beck, sports editor of the *Daily Local News* in West Chester." So, I'm hitless in two at-bats with the Phillies—or more bluntly, two rejections. I was getting itchy for more sports and less city news stories, so I began sending resumes to other newspapers. I landed two interviews in the same day, *Daily Local News* for Beck's former position and *The Wilmington News-Journal* sports department. The result? Two more rejections.

Then a break came my way. The person *The News-Journal* hired left after one week, and I was offered the job, covering high school sports in the state of Delaware. I joined the staff the first week in January 1963. Al Cartwright was the sports editor and Hal Bodley the assistant. Cartwright was demanding and critical. He worked in the day, so I seldom saw him. He would leave notes in my mailbox: "Baron von Shenk: You spelled [the school] Smyrna wrong. Damn it, get it right!" Every note or assignment was targeted for "Baron von Shenk." I became known as the Baron for the rest of my life.

One day, the mailbox note said, "You're covering the Phillies season opener." My nerves kicked in big time. The Phillies were playing the Cincinnati Reds at Connie Mack Stadium on Tuesday, April 9, Pete Rose's first road game. I introduced myself to Rose pregame and said, "I hope we're both around this game for a long time." Rose just nodded. Being a rookie writer from a suburban newspaper, I didn't feel as if I got treated well by Beck. I seemed to be invisible and I remembered that. While I was seated on the first-base side of the press box, a rookie broadcaster was in the Phillies booth on the third base side. Making his debut alongside Saam and Bill Campbell was Richie Ashburn. He turned out to be the most entertaining broadcaster in Phillies history.

The Phillies won, and Art Mahaffey pitched well. After the game the writers went to Gene Mauch's small office. I stood at the back of the pack and didn't say a word. When the pack peeled off, I approached Mauch and said, "Art won 19 games last year. Does he appear on track for another great season?" Gene stared at me and finally barked, "Why don't you go and ask him?"

Despite that rough treatment from Mauch, that week turned out to be a great one in my young life. The Phillies game was on Tuesday, and my wedding to Julie was on Saturday, April 13. Rather than a big wedding, Julie and I agreed on a small one with just the family. The honeymoon was one night in Washington, D.C. I couldn't find the hotel, but I appropriately found the ballpark. "That figures," said my new bride.

Fast forward to October. Bodley and I are the only ones left in the sports department after the morning paper was put to bed. "Baron, the Phillies PR job is open," Bodley said. "Why don't you apply? I think you could do the job." Though it was always my dream to work for the Phillies, I was apprehensive. They had three different public relations people in three seasons. Was it the person or the organization? I felt I was really learning under Bodley and Cartwright. But my dream had always been to work for the Phillies.

If I failed, there were always newspapers or teaching. I discussed the idea with Cartwright, and he encouraged me but said he couldn't promise taking me back if I failed or disliked my time with the Phillies. After sending in my application, I had an interview with Frank Powell, Phillies director of sales. He offered me the job on the spot, but I said I needed to discuss it with my new bride and I was looking for more money. "Here's a dime, call her on the pay phone," Powell said. After telling him that I needed to sit down with her, he consented and asked me to call as soon as possible.

Julie and I chatted, and she responded, "Why are you asking? You've already made up your mind." Her concern was that she would become a baseball widow, and that weighed on my mind as well. Living in a small apartment, we had only one car, and she would be alone for long hours at a time. Driving from south Wilmington, Delaware, to Connie Mack Stadium in north Philadelphia every day was not a quick trip. But it was an opportunity I couldn't turn down, and she understood that.

CHAPTER 9
A ROUGH ROOKIE SEASON

October 23, 1963, was my first day on the job. My salary was $7,000 plus a profit bonus of $1,000. I don't remember getting the bonus. If I didn't, can I collect interest on it? The player's average salary then was $14,400. Rookies and I had something in common. It certainly wasn't our compensation, but we were both living a dream.

Up one flight of stairs near the Connie Mack Stadium office entrance on 21st Street was a small office with a big metal desk, black metal cabinet, a huge green IBM typewriter, and a phone with four buttons. A concrete beam was overhead, about six and half feet from the floor. At 6'0" tall I barely cleared it when standing. George Fletcher, one of the Phillies' top-level executives, was in the next office. It was just the two of us in one isolated area behind home plate. President Bob Carpenter, general manager John Quinn, the farm director, and a secretary had offices on the same level but at third base. On the opposite side and same level were Frank Powell, Tom Hudson, and Frank Sullivan of the sales department. Ray Krise and the ticket office were also on the first-base side but on ground level. The accounting department was housed in the round tower behind home plate on the third floor. To get to Carpenter, Quinn, and the farm director, one had to take to the main concourse and head for third base.

I went to baseball's winter meetings at the El Cortez Hotel in San Diego that December. It was my first commercial flight. I didn't know a soul at the public relations meetings and had no idea what they were talking about. "We need all your information for the Green Book and Blue Book," we were told. Both publications were foreign to me, but I found out soon.

Quinn and manager Gene Mauch kept to themselves. I wasn't part of their company. Little did I know they were working on a major deal that would be my first announcement. Andy Seminick, manager of the Phillies' Chattanooga, Tennessee, affiliate, and Paul (Pope) Owens, then a scout based in Bakersfield, California, were also there. Owens must have known how out of place I felt. He took to me, and it was the start of a lifelong friendship. He offered me a drink. I remember saying, "I don't know what to order." He responded, "Seagram 7 and 7UP. Just tell the bartender you want a 14." As I was about to experience in my early years, there was considerable drinking in the game. I vowed not to get caught up with that. I couldn't risk losing my job over alcohol.

Listening to Seminick and Owens talk baseball was priceless. In the wee hours one morning, they got into a debate over the proper technique of the hook slide. We were in the empty lobby, and Owens runs and slides feet first into a sofa and declared, "Andy, that's how it should be done!"

Back in the office after the meetings, Quinn told me we were trading Don Demeter and Jack Hamilton to the Detroit Tigers for Jim Bunning and Gus Triandos. It was my first trade announcement. We didn't have a press conference; we just called the Associated Press (AP) and United Press International (UPI) wire services and four writers, Allen Lewis (*The Philadelphia Inquirer*), Ray Kelly (*Evening Bulletin*), Stan Hochman (*Philadelphia Daily News*), and Al Cartwright (*The Wilmington News-Journal*).

The Phillies were the only big league team without a media guide. When I inquired about it, I was told that it was too costly and that it was unnecessary. That didn't stop me. My wife, Julie, and I made 360 media guides by hand, which were approximately 8" x 4" horizontal. Using a red magic marker, she colored a Phillies hat on the covers. The text was printed by a mimeograph

Not permitted to publish a media guide in 1964, Julie and I made 360 copies of the guide, which served as the first of its kind for the Phillies.

machine. We cut the paper and punched two holes for binding purposes. Our living room floor was virtually unlivable for a few days. The next year I went ahead and printed a 40-page guide (5" x 7") through a printer without asking. The invoice for 1,000 guides was $1,425.

Spring Training

The Phillies trained at Jack Russell Stadium in Clearwater, Florida. Five of us from the front office, Mauch, coaches, writers, broadcasters, and players stayed at the Jack Tar Hotel (also known as the Fort Harrison Hotel). We didn't need alarm clocks because every morning at 6 AM, a train went through downtown Clearwater, blowing its whistle at every street intersection.

I was given a suite, which also was my office, and had a card table and my personal manual typewriter since there were no offices at Jack Russell Stadium. I had the suite for a reason. Every day after practice or games, the front office, Mauch, and his coaches, the broadcasters, and writers would gather there for a happy hour called the Cheese Room. There was discussion and sometimes heated debates on baseball, but most often the subject was golf...and more golf. Did I say golf? My job was to supply the booze and snacks. I'd go shopping at the ABC liquor store on Gulf-To-Bay Boulevard once a week. Not for bottles—but cases. Several times a week, I'd shop at Winn-Dixie, a grocery store. Crackers, cheese, more crackers, more cheese, more crackers...you get the idea. One time the cashier said, "You must be having some kind of a party." All the liquor and goodies were stored in my suite. There were four bellmen, and one was assigned each day to take the goodies from my room to the Cheese Room and back.

One of the bellman was named Buster. Believing that some of his players were violating his midnight curfew, Mauch gave Buster a baseball. "Get me some autographs after midnight, Buster," he instructed him. The next day Mauch fined four players for breaking curfew. In those days the hotel closed for the summer months. When our daughter was a year or two old, she spilled her bottle of milk on the coffee table in the suite on the last day of spring training. Some of the milk ran down the side of the table onto one of the four legs. We came back the next spring, got the same suite, and there was the milk stain on the table.

The copying machine was in the hotel sales office and available for us to use. There was a ticket office at the stadium, but it was open only when we played home games. We carried tickets with us and gave them away…or tried to give them away. We printed poster schedules, and I went to businesses, asking them to display them in their windows. One thing I learned that first spring was that the Clearwater Bombers, a professional men's softball team, was more popular than the Phillies. The Bombers played their games at Jack Russell Stadium, too. In the windows of businesses, we were competing against the Bombers.

We hired a local photographer to take black and white head shots and we needed 10 of each player. Julie would write the name of the player on the back, and I mailed them to the newspapers back north. Newspapers wouldn't send photographers to spring training until later years.

Practices took all day because we had only one field at the stadium. Prior to Jack Russell Stadium, the Phillies played there when it was Athletic Field. But by 1964 there was no evidence that a grandstand once existed. It was a plain old baseball field in such bad condition that it was nicknamed Iwo Jima. Rookies got to work out there most of the time. Right field was very short (290'), which meant a lot of baseballs were lost during batting practice. Neighborhood kids would stand on the other side of that fence and cart off dozens of baseballs.

I wasn't the lone newbie in camp. Among the rookies were Rick Wise, Johnny Briggs, and someone named Richie Allen, who moved to third base, a position he hadn't played since high school. Veteran Don Hoak, a former Marine, was the incumbent. I can still see him standing behind Allen at third base during batting practice with his arms folded across his chest and a mean glare, watching every move of the young slugger. A young athlete was taking a job from an aging veteran. We didn't keep track of spring training stats in those days, but Allen put on some kind of display. He hit something like 12 to 15 homers. I remember a towering blast at Al Lopez Field in Tampa. The ball hit the lights in the left-field light tower. If it hadn't hit the lights, it might have landed in Pasco County.

Almost everyone had a car except rookies, which meant, of course, I didn't have a car. I either walked to the stadium or hitched a ride. That was the case for dinner, too, and there weren't many dining options in Clearwater back then—just a coffee shop and a restaurant in the hotel, Jimmy Hall's steak house about four blocks away, and the Beachcomber on Clearwater Beach. Every night Phillies officials, writers, and broadcasters dined at the latter. Entertaining the media was part of my job. I must have put on 20 pounds that first spring feasting on shrimp cocktail, steak, and baked Alaska. That weight is still there. Finally, Cartwright told Carpenter, "For God's sake, Bob, get Larry a car." When he finally gave me one, I drove two or three writers to road games.

I'll never forget the first home game. Cookie Rojas was our first batter. He grounded to the pitcher, who threw the ball over the first baseman's head. I stood up and yelled, "Go, Cookie, Go." Lewis, who would become a mentor and a lifelong friend, grabbed me by the belt, and yanked me back in the metal folding chair. "First rule: no cheering in the press box. Understand?"

The press box was an open area behind home plate and under a metal roof. Pigeons nested in the beams supporting the roof. My daily job was to clean the press box table top of pigeon crap. The glory of working for a professional baseball team, eh? Not all writers sat in the press box. There was a grassy area at the end of the first-base stands. Three or four writers would park themselves there and take off their shirts to get a tan. Most of the writers were on the beefy side. We named the area "Whale Beach" and had a sign erected on the fence. Years later bleacher seats were installed in the area—much to the dismay of the Whale Beach inhabitants. To preserve the peace, railings were installed to box in an area that became the new Whale Beach.

Writers typed their stories on brown copy paper and then handed their stories to a Western Union operator who would key in the story to the newspaper. Most of the time, Western Union had an operator in the press box. Sometimes the writers (or me) had to deliver the stories to Western Union's office in downtown Clearwater. Many a time, Kelly would leave in the middle of the game for the racetrack in Tampa, Florida. He'd say to me, "Hey, big boy, write in the final score and give it to the operator."

The Regular Season

I decided to type one page of standings and probable pitchers, one page of stats, and one page of something I called "Newsy Notes." One writer sarcastically wrote, "The Newsy Notes certainly aren't newsy." That's okay. I outlasted that writer. I vowed I would outlast those that were difficult to get along with.

One time early in the season, Lewis handed me the page with the standings. He had circled a lot of mistakes with a red pen. "You need to be more accurate, Baron," he sternly advised. I just smiled, "Allen, I copied them from *your* newspaper."

I recorded stats of each player in an 8" x 11" notebook. Red meant road games, and blue meant home. I never found anything from previous seasons I could simulate. I did find diaries from years past, which included a box score, standings, and a note or two from that particular day. So I continued that tradition. The book from the 1963 season I located was only half-filled.

I didn't travel with the team often. At first, I would type one page of Phillies stats and give them to Lewis to put in the press box of the first road game. The rest of the trip, we had nothing, so writers and broadcasters had to keep their own stats. Later we paid Lewis to type stats for the first game of every road series. A couple of teams (the Pittsburgh Pirates and the Los Angeles Dodgers) had their traveling secretary type the stats on the road. When those teams came to Connie Mack Stadium, their traveling secretary paid me $20 a game to type their stat sheet. That money meant a lot in those days.

During the middle of the season, Bunning, the player rep, came to me with a request: no more radio interviews unless the players get paid. I was young and naïve and couldn't believe players got gifts for doing pregame and postgame Phillies shows. Players got points for those appearances and at the end of the season, the station (WFIL) gave them a catalogue from which they could select gifts. But Bunning wasn't talking about those interviews. With increased media attention, more radio reporters were on hand with their tape recorders, getting sound bites. Bunning felt interviews enhanced the shows, which had sponsors. We settled that players would do radio interviews as long as they were no longer than a minute.

My first road trip was Houston, Los Angeles, and San Francisco just before the All-Star Game. We got to L.A. from Houston in the wee hours of the morning, which is quite normal on the road. We picked up our room keys in the Ambassador Hotel lobby and headed for our rooms. I couldn't find mine and went back to the front desk. The hotel also had individual cottages on the property, and I was assigned to one of them. I walked in to see a living room, two bedrooms, small kitchen, two bathrooms, and a large dining table bigger than our apartment back in Wilmington. In the middle of the table was a big basket of fruit, "Mr. Carpenter, on behalf of the Ambassador Hotel management, welcome." I didn't tell anyone. With a two-game series against the Dodgers, my luxurious living only lasted two nights.

Coming back from that trip, we were in first place, and I couldn't have been more excited. The town was buzzing about the Phillies for the first time since 1950. Would this finally be another World Series?

Mauch would try double switches, platoons, pinch-hitters, defensive replacements, hit-and-runs, squeeze plays, and it all worked. He loved to bunt early and get on the scoreboard first. Allen and Johnny Callison provided the long ball. Bobby Wine, Ruben Amaro, Tony Taylor, and Rojas anchored the middle infield. Of that quartet only Taylor was used at one position. Bunning was a sensation in his first season. Chris Short was a solid No. 2 starter, and Jack Baldschun closed games.

The year, 1964, seemed to be our time. Bunning threw a perfect game on Father's Day. I was doing my weekend duty with the Delaware Air National Guard and didn't see the game. A month later Callison won the All-Star Game with a dramatic ninth-inning home run and was named MVP. He's the only All-Star MVP the Phillies ever had. I saw that game as a spectator and saw the homer while standing at the back of the lower stands. We made the cover of *Sports Illustrated* on August 10 with a headline: "Philadelphia's Johnny Callison. Pennant Fever After 14 Years." Triandos called it the year of the Blue Snow.

Heading down the stretch, we're up by six and a half games with 12 to go. It was nearly mathematically impossible to lose the pennant. I was flying as high as the fans but needed to remind myself I had a job to do, which included planning the press box seating, auxiliary press box seating, credentials,

I pose with right fielder Johnny Callison, one of my many friends on the 1964 Phillies. No, I don't have that sport coat anymore.

broadcast booths, World Series program, hospitality functions, etc. My head was spinning. Powell and I went to the Warwick Hotel. We needed the ballroom for a potential World Series party on a Saturday night. The hotel GM said, "Sorry, but it is booked for a wedding reception." Powell asked, "Where's [the hotel owner] Fred Mann?" We found out he was on vacation in Paris. Powell plowed ahead anyway. "Get him on the phone," he said. We did, and Mann tossed the wedding reception. I left thinking, *wow, the power of the big leagues is pretty impressive.*

While our hotel plans went right, everything on the field started to go wrong. "For 150 games I could stumble over home plate, and it would turn into two runs," Mauch said. Then the Phillies lost 10 in a row. Up until then our longest losing streak was four games, which happened only three times. We were so busy preparing for a World Series, it was a blur. It all actually began to unravel on September 19 in Los Angeles. Tied 3–3 after 15 innings, the Dodgers won it with two out in the last of the 16th when Willie Davis stole home. Bunning won the next day, our last win of the month. When the team returned home around 12:30 AM, something like 2,000 giddy fans welcomed their heroes.

Monday, September 21, at Philadelphia
- Reds 1, Phillies 0. Chico Ruiz stole home in the sixth inning with Frank Robinson at bat for the lone run. Twice in three games, we lost because of steals of home. That is unheard of. But the magic number remained at seven.

Tuesday, September 22, at Philadelphia
- Reds 9, Phillies 2. Starter Chris Short gave up six runs. The magic number didn't change. Earlier that day World Series tickets went on sale through the mail, and 52,000 requests were delivered to the ticket office the following morning.

Wednesday, September 23, at Philadelphia
- Reds 6, Phillies 4. Vada Pinson's three-run homer in a six-run seventh was the game-winner. An uneasiness began to creep into the picture as the lead shrank to three and a half games with nine left.

Thursday, September 24, at Philadelphia
- Braves 5, Phillies 3. Bunning gave up three runs in six innings for the loss. The lead was now down to three games.

Friday, September 25, at Philadelphia
- Braves 7, Phillies 5, 12 innings. This was a real gut-wrencher on a night that turned out to be Black Friday. The Phillies led 1–0 until the top of the seventh when Denis Menke reached base on catcher's interference, not a common occurance. Two runs in that inning and one in the

eighth put Milwaukee up 3–1. Callison tied the game with a two-run homer in their turn at-bat. In the 10th the Braves scored twice for another two-run lead. But Allen hit a two-out, two-run, inside-the-park home run in our 10th. Once again, the Braves put up another two-run inning, but we couldn't match it in our 12th inning at-bat. Still we led the Cincinnati Reds by two and a half games and the Cardinals by two.

Saturday, September 26, at Philadelphia

- Braves 6, Phillies 4. Leading 4–3 in the top of the ninth, a sure win turned into a bitter loss on Rico Carty's three-run triple that hit the right-field chalk line and proved to be the game-winner. Another inch, and it's a foul ball, and the Phillies would have won. Callison was ill with a severe case of the flu but refused to come out of the lineup. The once jubilant fans began to boo.

Sunday, September 27, at Philadelphia

- Braves 14, Phillies 8 in the final home game. Callison, still ill, hit three homers, but the Braves got seven runs on 10 hits in three innings off Bunning. The Phillies dropped to second place for the first time since July 16, a period of 73 days. With intensified booing the players were glad to get out of town. Cincinnati was now in first place, and the Cardinals were one and a half games out. Callison was 8-for-18 with four homers and nine RBIs in the four-game series against the Braves. Had we hung on to win the pennant, he would have been the National League's MVP.

Monday, September 28, at St. Louis

- Cardinals 5, Phillies 1. Bob Gibson was simply too much, dropping us into third place. After the game our clubhouse remained closed for 20 minutes. Before the game, Mauch held a meeting, according to the book, *Jim Bunning, Baseball and Beyond.* "He just tried to enrage us," Bunning said. "He said, 'You're letting it slip away, letting somebody take it away from you. Go start a fight. Do something.'"

Tuesday, September 29, at St. Louis

- Cardinals 4, Phillies 2. The Reds lost, putting them in a first-place tie with the Cardinals. Callison, weakened by the flu, didn't start but did get a pinch-hit single and begged to stay in the game. When he got to first base, he asked for a jacket. Unable to fasten the zipper and pull it up, St. Louis first baseman Bill White came to the rescue.

Wednesday, September 30, at St. Louis

- Cardinals 8, Phillies 5. The Phillies fell two and a half games back. According to a 1965 *Sports Illustrated* article, Mauch was spotted sitting on a green bench in his bullpen during batting practice. St. Louis shortstop Dick Groat said: "No one could possibly imagine what he has gone through or what is going through his mind now."

Thursday, October 1, open date

- The records were: Cardinals 92–67, Reds 92–68, Phillies 90–70, and Giants 89–70.

Friday, October 2, at Cincinnati

- Phillies 4, Reds 3. The Phillies ended their skid by scoring all four of their runs in the eighth.

Saturday, October 3, open date

- The Cardinals and Reds (92–69) were tied, and the Phillies were one game back (91–70).

Sunday, October 4, at Cincinnati

- Phillies 10, Reds 0. Bunning threw a six-hitter. New York's Galen Cisco led the Cardinals, and it was 3–2, going into the bottom of the fifth. The Cardinals scored three in the fifth, sixth, and eighth. According to a *Sports Illustrated* article written by Steve Wulf, Mauch was in the visitors' clubhouse after the final win, trying to pick up the Mets-Cardinals game on the radio. "When White hit the homer, I knew it was over," Mauch told Wulf.

- "I remember the atmosphere in the clubhouse," Ruben Amaro commented in Bunning's book. "It was like everybody sat stunned, I mean for an endless time." Bunning added, "I didn't say anything to anybody. Nobody said anything to anybody. It was a total blah. We were out of it. We had it. It was ours. And we let go." A once-promising season had ended bitterly. Rojas told *Sports Illustrated* the collapse was "like swimming in a long, long lake, and then you drown."

- "We all must have been tired. I didn't feel tired because of the adrenaline, but I must have been," Bunning said in his book. "We all must have been because we all played bad. Our defense, which had been unbelievably good for 150 games, was terrible. When we pitched good, we didn't hit. When we hit good, we didn't pitch. We had our losing streak at the wrong time of the year."

Had the Cardinals lost, a first-ever round-robin playoffs (double-elimination) would have started the next day with the Reds at Phillies followed by the Cardinals at Reds on Tuesday and the Phillies at Cardinals on Wednesday. All of us in the front office were on alert. If the playoffs were to start the day after the season ended, we were told to be prepared to come to the ballpark Sunday night and work all night. The phone call never came.

Knowing we needed just one win, Mauch started Bunning and Short on two days rest, and it backfired. Critics blamed Mauch for losing the pennant. I don't. If it hadn't been for Mauch's managing, we wouldn't even have been in a position to win.

The four-color cover for the World Series program was printed. (We ended up using that cover for the 1966 Yearbook.) Tickets were printed. A bulldozer stood by waiting to move ground by both dugouts to make room for additional field-level seats. But there would be no World Series. The 10-game losing streak and lost pennant lived with the organization for years. It was a bitter pill to swallow. As the years passed, whenever another team had a lead late in the season and began losing, the media would call for information on the 10-game losing streak and want to talk to guys on the 1964 team. Mauch did not want to review that season for the media. The players got tired of talking about it, too. Rojas informed me, "If you get any more calls, don't bother calling me."

"The 1964 club was still a young one," Wine said. "But Gene looked at the talent and drilled us on playing the game the right way. We hit a spell where things didn't go well. We wouldn't execute like we did all year." Known for his intensity that could lead to verbal explosions, Mauch was different during the losing streak. "He was calm," Wine said. "He didn't want to look like he was panicking. Just said, 'Let's get 'em.'" Dalrymple echoed the sentiment about Mauch's guidance. "The one thing I kept waiting for was an explosion from Mauch," Dalrymple said. "He was so calm through the losing streak."

Perhaps the baseball gods had been disturbed. A few players were making plans to bring family members to Philadelphia for the World Series. Some were spending the anticipated World Series checks. In August, Sandy Koufax was supposed to start against us at home. We called the game because of potential rain which never came. The game was rescheduled for September 8 on Yom Kippur, the holy Jewish day when Koufax wouldn't start. Frank Thomas broke his right thumb that night, a critical blow to us. Were the baseball gods getting even?

A young team, however, bonded that year. They've remained close ever since. The 25th reunion was a fun time for them, including for Mauch. He told Wulf, "You know, I've talked to them more in the last two days than I did in any two years as manager. I have a deep, deep feeling about this team. I did then, too, but I was hard on them because I felt that was the way to go. This weekend has given me a chance to tell them exactly how I feel and to thank them. It felt great being a part of the '64 Phillies again."

Ed Roebuck, one of the few veterans on the team, attended the reunion. "I have nothing but good memories of this uniform. I've heard all the excuses over and over that we'd won if Gene hadn't started Bunning and Short so often, or if Chico Ruiz hadn't gone on his own, or if Frank Thomas hadn't been hurt, or—this one is real bull—if I hadn't been hurt. But Gene did a tremendous job that year. He got the most out of us, and people forget he was so young at the time. I think, plain and simple, that we were a good club that wasn't good enough, and the fact that we got so close was a tribute to him."

CHAPTER 10

THE OFFSEASON, SPRING TRAINING, AND OPENING DAY

As we were nearing the final season of Connie Mack Stadium, I got up the nerve to request an audience with Bob Carpenter, the owner and president. My concern was that we needed to change the way we were doing business. There were more seats to fill at Veterans Stadium. Promotions and public relations needed a big change, and we needed to increase our staff. When I left his office, I wasn't sure I made any impact.

But following the 1969 season came a surprise announcement, Bill Giles was joining the Phillies as vice president, business operations. He was going to oversee promotions, tickets, PR, sales, marketing, broadcasting, advertising, ballpark operations—the entire business end—and help us move smoothly into our new home, Veterans Stadium. He was precisely what we needed.

Our uniform that had been in play since 1950 changed as we approached the Vet. Numbers were added on the front of the jersey, a new "P" 6½ inches tall adorned the left side of the jersey, a ⅞-inch bold burgundy stripe ran down each side of the jersey and pants, the name Phillies was removed but pinstripes remained. We held a press conference late in 1969 to unveil the new uniforms with players as the models. Promotions and PR were going full force to change our image. Usherettes at the new home, called Fillies, were part of the new look. The front office staff expanded. (As I can best recall, there were 15 in the office when I started in 1963.) Al Cartwright took a leave of absence from *The Wilmington News-Journal* to help in PR.

In January of 1970, we started a press caravan that became a yearly ritual and the responsibility of my department. Create goodwill, sell tickets, and increase the fan base were the goals of the caravan. Over time we became popular throughout eastern Pennsylvania, southern New Jersey, and Delaware. We'd board a bus at the Vet on a Monday morning, spend the week doing two appearances a day in the tri-state area, stay overnight in various towns, and return to Philadelphia on Friday night. Exhausted is the proper adjective.

The general manager, manager, Giles, Harry Kalas, four to five players, our promotions director, somebody from sales and group sales, and I made the yearly journeys. Giles felt fans needed to see the players up close and personal. Greg Luzinski, Larry Bowa, Bob Boone, Mike Schmidt, Garry Maddox, Tim McCarver, Pete Rose, and Larry Christenson were among the many players who participated in the early years. We'd present a program for the Lions, Kiwanis, and Rotary clubs; church groups; network radio stations' sponsors; etc. We'd give away door prizes, which were usually autographed items from the players. For years we would show our highlight film as part of the program. Some years we would mix in school visits or visits to hospitals.

I remember being at a high school in Freehold, New Jersey, one winter. Players were on a stage, taking questions from students. One student asked Rose if he ever went to college. Rose replied, "You mean to tell me you've been sitting here for a half hour and can't tell I ain't never been to no college?" Visiting a vet hospital in Allentown one year proved too shocking for Glenn Wilson. He couldn't handle seeing the disabled vets and had to exit early. Wilson was a tough Texan but not this time. Luzinski picked up a baby on one of the stops and kissed it. The local newspaper next day had the photo on the front page. Organist Paul Richardson was part of the traveling party. He'd provide musical entertainment to the programs. Fans loved him. A local music store would provide an organ or piano for him.

While in Lancaster, Pennsylvania, to start the 1974 caravan, Kalas introduced Dave Cash as our new second baseman. We had acquired him from the Pittsburgh Pirates for Ken Brett the previous October in an unpopular move. Cash approached the microphone, froze, and sat down. I'm thinking, *Geez, this guy can't talk*. He turned out to be the club's vocal leader. He coined the phrase, "Yes We Can" and was instrumental in us becoming a championship-caliber team. Cash turned out to be a three-time All-Star and the last Phillies player to have back-to-back 200-hit seasons. Once again, Paul Owens knew what he was doing.

Staying overnight sometimes became adventurous. In Lancaster one time, we were in the bar celebrating Owens' birthday. The hotel brought a cake. A fan kept pestering him. Owens handed the cake to the fan, moved it in front of the fan's face, and then smashed it into his face. Topping it off he took some icing on his finger and stuck it in the guy's right ear. The fan was livid, claimed he was an FBI agent, and said he would track Owens forever. It took Luzinski and Bowa a long time to calm down the guy.

We were in Harrisburg, Pennsylvania, on the last night of the week-long journey. The date was January 17, 1991. During the program we learned the United States had launched Operation Desert Storm against Iraq. Our program that night was subdued, and afterward we headed for the bus quickly. Since I was in charge, I told the bus driver, "Let's go" without counting noses. We all wanted to hear the news. A couple of hours later we arrived at the Vet. Foster Mears, the night watchman, said, "Baron, you left Paul Richardson in Harrisburg. He's at this phone number and he's not very happy." The phone number was the Reading airport terminal, which didn't make sense. Turns out Paul had left his wallet on our bus. He had no money, no credit card, no driver's license, and couldn't rent a car. He bummed a ride from a fan that was going from Harrisburg to the Reading airport. Foster termed Richardson's state of mind as "not very happy." That was totally inaccurate. He was livid. I made the mistake, so I drove to Reading and found one person sitting in the terminal, Richardson. The ride back to the Vet was basically speechless. I got home at around 3 AM.

Spring Training

The best part of the baseball calendar: leaving the gray, cold north of Philadelphia for six to seven weeks in Clearwater, Florida! Spring training came in three phases—can't wait to get there, can't wait to start playing the games, and can't wait to get the season started. Although spring training was an enjoyable time in my mind, it wasn't always that for others. Players complained that it was too long. Perhaps that is correct, but it takes time and weeks for a pitcher to get his arm in shape. Hitters can do it more quickly.

One time John Quinn was called away just before the Opening Day ceremonies were to begin at Jack Russell Stadium. I was told to stand in for him and say a few words. My usual pregame job was to play a recording of the national anthem on an old record player in the press box. Bill Hammitt was the public address announcer, so I told him he had to do it. He got nervous and butchered it, playing the anthem at the wrong—and very slow—speed. It must have taken four minutes.

Bill White was rehabbing from surgery for a torn Achilles tendon that occurred after the 1966 season. While aggressively working out at first base, he let out a yell and fell to the ground. Blood was oozing from his torn stitches. Angry at himself for pushing himself too hard to get on the field, he hobbled into the Jack Russell clubhouse, lay down on the concrete, and pounded his fists on the floor. He screamed, "You dummy, you dummy, you dummy."

Another time *Sports Illustrated* wanted to take a photo of Rose sliding headfirst into third base. The photographer would lie on the ground to get a unique angle. My concern was that if Rose got injured, we'd all be in serious trouble. Rose was willing to do it, so I permitted *SI* to do the shot, but it had to be only two takes. Two days later the photographer called. The camera had malfunctioned, and he wanted to try it again. *Oh, boy,* I thought. I approached Rose, and he responded: "Big magazine, ain't it?" So, we did it again, but I allowed only one slide. I was nervous. The photo turned out to be spectacular. *SI* gave me a print, and Rose signed it for me, "To Baron."

During spring training of 1981, players and front office staff were told to be in the Carpenter Field clubhouse first thing one morning as Ruly Carpenter wanted to meet with everyone. Chris Wheeler asked, "Baron, what's up? Do you know anything?" I had no idea but jokingly said, "Maybe he's selling the team." That indeed was the shocking message. Nobody knew in advance, not even Owens, Giles, or Dallas Green.

Many years later Tug McGraw would come to camp as a guest instructor. In 2003 he became ill and was admitted to Morton Plant Hospital in Clearwater. The media was eager to know what was wrong and updates. I met with the PR staff at the hospital. We decided any comments would come from the club—not the hospital or doctors. There was something seriously wrong with McGraw, but we didn't want to say much pending his family's wishes. Then his son, musician Tim McGraw, came to the hospital. He now was the decision-maker and the point man for any information.

One thing that differs between spring training and the regular season is what happens when a starting pitcher or starting player leaves the game. In the spring the media can go to the clubhouse to interview the pitcher and any other player out of the game. Some starting pitchers have routines to follow, so a PR person needs to know that, monitor his routine, and let the media know when that particular pitcher is available. For home games it wasn't too difficult because there are usually a couple of PR persons on hand. Road games were different. Usually one person makes the trip. That person sits in the press box and monitors the changes that are being made in addition to maintaining the spring training scorebook. So once a starting pitcher left a game, the media left the press box for the clubhouse, and the PR person remained anchored in the press box.

I got in hot water one time when the Phillies were playing the Kansas City Royals in Haines City, Florida. Curt Schilling started and left the game, the media went to the clubhouse, and I stayed in the press box. Schilling and pitching coach Galen Cisco were in the middle of a loud and heated argument when the scribes strolled in. Terry Francona was the manager and he wasn't too happy with me. From then on a PR person had to be in the clubhouse first before the media—home or road.

In the early years, the front office stayed in the Jack Tar Hotel or Fort Harrison Hotel. (It had multiple names at one time.) Then we moved to the Sandcastle Motel on Drew Street and eventually the Holiday Inn on Route 19. The Holiday Inn cleared out three sleeping rooms on ground level just off the lobby entrance and restaurant for office space. Baseball administration (Tony Siegle and Susan Ingersoll) had an office in one room and a conference room in the next. Wheeler and I had the first room. All the normal hotel room furniture was removed. Desks and temporary ceiling lights were brought in. We'd go to the office first thing in the morning, then to Jack Russell Stadium for the workout or game, and then back to the Holiday Inn for the rest of the day. Ingersoll never got to see a game as she remained at the hotel all day. By being in the first room, Wheeler and I had all kinds of visitors. People would walk in and ask: "Where's the ice machine?" "How far is St. Petersburg from here?" "Do you have shuttle service to the airport?" "Where is room 333?" I can't blame them. They saw an office and figured it was part of the Holiday Inn. Without cell phones, it was difficult to communicate with Ingersoll at the Holiday Inn and the rest of us at the stadium or Carpenter Field where there were no phones. One spring, we got beepers for all of us, but adjacent to Carpenter Field was an incinerator plant, and trash trucks were always going in and out. When the trucks backed up, you heard "beep, beep, beep." Owens would hear the beeps and talk into the beeper, not realizing there was no one on the other end. We had a few laughs about that. In the early 1970s, we were allowed to live outside a hotel at condos on the beach or houses that could be rented.

In 1984 we put a minor league team in Clearwater. Offices at Jack Russell Stadium were upgraded for the Clearwater staff. When spring training came, we moved into those offices, and the Clearwater staff moved to a building in the left-field corner. Currently, the Phillies have the best facilities in Florida and first-class offices at Bright House Field.

First Spring Training Memories

Larry Andersen "That was 1972, and you want me to remember what? Heck, I can't remember where I left my shoes when I get up every morning. Well, it was in Tucson, Arizona, and I was one of many minor leaguers with the Indians. We stayed at the Flamingo Hotel. At least I think so. I don't remember my roommate. But I do remember my number, 112...I think. I was nervous and scared and—after one day— fighting blisters from the Kangaroo spikes. What did I like? Absolutely nothing. I grew up in [the state of] Washington, so the warm weather was nice. But I couldn't handle the Arizona heat. I really struggled, especially all that running. I hated mornings. Getting up early and riding a bus for a few hours, that wasn't fun. I slept through most of the bus rides. Matter of fact, I slept through most of my spring trainings, which was rather apparent if you saw me pitch. I do remember being in the Mariners big league camp in 1981. Maury Wills was the manager. There was another pitcher in camp who looked like me—or so they say—Brian Allard. He was five years younger, so I don't know how we looked alike. I guess it was because we both had hair. Anyway, Maury got us mixed up. He'd call me Brian, and him Larry. I was having a great spring, which was unusual. Brian was having a terrible spring. I was stressed out that Maury would pick him because he called him Larry. Happy ending, though. I made the club."

Jack Baldschun "My first camp was with the Reds minor leagues in 1961 in Douglas, Georgia. My most vivid memory from that first year didn't take place in uniform. I was from the North and experienced segregation for the first time. It was difficult to understand how blacks were treated. The next year, I was in the Phillies camp in Clearwater. I wanted to be a starter; Gene Mauch wanted me as the closer. I remember saying, 'Let me start every fifth day, and in between I can relieve.' As you know, Gene didn't go for it. Spring training was fun, being away from the winter, being in a warm climate, and being with your teammates. I also enjoyed the fun we had with other families."

Ricky Bottalico "My first spring was 1992 with the Phillies minor leaguers. I lived in a small apartment near the bay with another pitcher, Dan Brown. I remember walking in the clubhouse at Carpenter Complex and seeing a No. 9 with my name on it hanging in a locker. I felt strange that first day because I really didn't know most of the minor leaguers, and there were a lot of them. I really loved spring training every year because I was getting out of cold weather and playing baseball. It was work, but it was fun work. I enjoyed the rare chances we had to play some golf. What didn't I like? My performance. I was a terrible, terrible spring training pitcher. I couldn't get anyone out."

Larry Bowa "First spring training was in Leesburg, Florida, 1966. We had three guys share a hotel room at the Leesburg hotel. We had food tickets and after breakfast we would walk to the ballpark. I began switch-hitting after the 1967 season in the instructional league. My roommates were Pat Bayless and Mel Roberts. I don't know my number, but I do know the wool uniforms were very uncomfortable during that time of year. The thing I remember most were the number of guys in camp. Knowing I was underrated, I figured the odds of me making a team weren't very good."

Marty Bystrom "It was 1978. I was 19 years old and with the Spartanburg Phillies. Forty-two was my uniform number, and my roommate was Manny Abreu. My fondest memory of the first day was how everyone threw so much harder than I did. I thought to myself,

Where did these guys come from? It was eye-opening for sure. I also felt so proud to put on the Phillies uniform. The thing I liked most was the challenge of facing hitters who were so much more experienced than I had faced in college. The things I liked the least was only getting soup and crackers for lunch and the Circle Jerk. We had to run in a circle in the outfield with glove in hand, full uniform, and wearing spikes for 20 minutes. On each lap a coach would hit a ground ball, so you had to bend down to field it. It was more of a mental conditioning process than physical."

Larry Christenson "It was 1973 with the Phillies in Clearwater. I was No. 51. Roy Thomas was my roomie. What I remember from that first day was the dozens of writers and media that were following Steve Carlton around like the Pied Piper. He had won 27 games the previous year, and I was wondering who this Carlton guy was. I enjoyed the sun, the fun, and competing for a spot on the team. I didn't like running because of my terribly bad back and the painful back spasms I would go through."

Pat Combs "I was invited to big league camp my first year out of Baylor University in 1989. I was so excited that I reported to camp early on February 12. Nobody was in the locker room, but I worked out anyway. My first number for camp was 45. My roommate was Jason Grimsley. My fondest memory was putting on my uniform for the first time. I don't think my feet ever hit the floor that day. It was like I was in a dream. I really enjoyed getting a chance to meet the coaches and players, who I had admired and watched play. I remember meeting Larry Bowa, thinking that I had watched him play against the Astros in the 1980 playoffs that still ranks as one of the best divisional playoff series in the history of baseball. I remember mentioning to Bo that I was 13 years old and in the Astrodome watching Game 5. He laughed and told me that it ranked as one of his fondest baseball memories. My first day of pitching live BP was a day I never forgot. The position players had just reported to camp, and we were pitching BP to them. The second hitter I faced was none other than Mike Schmidt. He was one of my baseball heroes. I always loved the way he played and approached the game. I was so pumped that I did not realize how hard I was throwing. I blew the first few pitches by him, and he was getting upset. He finally yelled out to me to 'Take a little off, rookie!' I was embarrassed and thought later that I had just 'showed up' a legend. The learning part of how to be a big leaguer was what I remember being a challenge. Some of the players were willing to help, and some just let you go to figure things out for yourself."

Clay Dalrymple "It was 1959 in Bradenton, Florida, with the Milwaukee Braves. Hank Aaron was the Rookie of the Year the year before, and I remember watching him taking BP in my first camp. He just sprayed line drives all over the field. Getting out of the cold weather in the North was what I liked the most about spring training. Being a catcher, I got there before the rest of the position players. Workouts for pitchers and catchers weren't as long, so I had time to get in some bass fishing. I didn't care for the 10 wind sprints every day, and the first few days of squatting left me with some very sore calf muscles and legs. It was hard to walk up steps for a few days."

Darren Daulton "I fell in love with Clearwater the first spring, 1981. I don't remember my uniform number. Heck, it might have been 125! I think Ken Dowell was my roommate. I was scared to death that first day but fit right in because everyone else in the clubhouse was scared. I enjoyed being able to work my rear end off while looking at palm trees. I thought I was in paradise. Conversely, I disliked looking at palm trees while working my rear end off."

Billy DeMars "It was 1947 with the Dodgers minor leaguers, and we trained at the Pensacola [Florida] Air Base. They had a large complex of baseball fields. We lived in barracks, and there were a ton of players. Back then the Dodgers had something like 26 minor league clubs, which amounted to 350 or 400 players. Every day they would blow a bugle at 6 AM. We'd pile out of bed and get in lines. We lined up for everything: breakfast, lunch, dinner, meetings, and heading to the workouts. I remember the first day. Wade Mathews would ride in a Jeep and blow a whistle every 15 minutes. That meant we had to jog around the fields. I don't remember my number, but we all had a paper number attached to the back of the uniform, and with 350 or 400 players, there were high numbers. My first spring with the Phillies was 1969 at Jack Russell Stadium. As a hitting coach, I loved working with the players in the cages. It never seemed like work. There was nothing I disliked about spring training. I just loved the game and was glad to be part of it."

Bob Dernier "I went from Double A to the majors in September 1980, so I hadn't been in a big league spring training camp before I got to the big leagues, which was kind of unique. The following year, I was in camp with the world champions at Jack Russell Stadium. It was exciting and at the same time somewhat intimidating. But Mike Schmidt, Pete Rose, and Tug McGraw made me feel like I belonged. I lived on the beach with Marty Bystrom and later with Von Hayes. The atmosphere of spring training was great—lots of fond times and memories. I'd wake up at six every morning and run on the beach for 30 minutes and get to the park about 7:30. I just loved that part. Not knowing if you were going to make a club or hearing trade rumors were things I didn't care for. In 1984 I was traded at the end of spring training. I was kind of down because when you get traded it's like you get divorced."

Lee Elia "It was with the Phillies minor league camp in 1959 in Kissimmee, Florida. I don't remember my uniform number, but it was up there in the 60s or 70s. I couldn't believe there were that many players in the camp, which really was for the Class A players only. We lived in a hotel, six to a room. If a roommate got released, someone else moved in. Growing up in Philadelphia and going to Florida every year was special. During the early years, we went south on the train. No more snow or cold weather—just sunshine, warm weather, palm trees, the smell of grass being cut, the sight of a baseball field. It meant the start of another season was at hand. I loved the game, so there was nothing I didn't like."

Bill Giles "When I was six years old, I went to spring training in Tampa with the Reds because my dad was the president of the Reds. The players stayed at the Floridian Hotel. Elevators in those days were manually operated with a wheel-like device. I spent a lot of time as the elevator operator. Eight years later I went with Dad to Clearwater for a Reds-Phillies game at Athletic Park. Robin Roberts pitched that day. I remember Dad saying, 'See that pitcher? He's going to be a great one some day.'"

Dallas Green "Bob Conley, Don Cardwell, Chris Short, and I were invited to a mini-camp before the big league camp opened in Clearwater. Short and I rode the train from Wilmington, Delaware. We stayed at the West Coast Hotel, three to a room. We weren't allowed to have cars, so we walked everywhere. We were kept around to throw BP to Hamner, Jones, Ennis, Ashburn, and those guys. We were young, wild, could throw hard, and we were trying to impress everyone. The vets hated us, didn't want to face us. Later I was sent to Bennettsville, South Carolina, where the Phillies low minor league players trained. I wore No. 177 or 176. The next year, I was drafted by the Army at the start of spring training. I thought my career was over before it started. I took a bus back to Philly for a physical exam. The following day, we were lined up to get on a bus for boot camp in South Carolina. Four of us were called out of line and taken into a little room. They told me I had failed my physical because of a hernia. So [it was] back on the bus for spring training. During the early days, you were always trying to impress someone. I was nervous, scared but excited to be rubbing elbows with Roberts and Simmons. In '56 the younger players used the old clubhouse at Athletic Field, the field we called Iwo Jima. We weren't allowed at Jack Russell Stadium. That old clubhouse was awful. You almost had to dress and shower in shifts. The hardest part was being sent down and having to pack and move. You might go from Clearwater to Plant City and then to Bennettsville or Leesburg."

Kevin Gross "It was 1981 with the Phillies in Clearwater. I don't recall my uniform number other than it was a high number. We stayed at the Days Inn. I don't remember my roomie, maybe Darren Daulton or Ed Wojna. I remember initially looking around at all the talent and saying to myself, 'I have no chance of making it to the majors, let alone the minors.' After several days I fit in pretty good and did well.

The knowledge of the coaches and instructors was impressive and appreciated. I had never been around anything like that before. Waking up each morning to compete for a spot on a team was what I liked the most. I really didn't have many things I didn't like about it. I guess one thing would have been a little more time to go fishing."

Cole Hamels "[In] 2003 at Carpenter Field, we stayed at the EconoLodge. My roommate was Vinny DeChristofaro. I believe my number was 79 or 80. I was excited about being in camp. The clubhouse was packed. It seemed like half of the players spoke Spanish. I was freshly shaved for the first day, showed up in shorts and sandals—what I usually wore in San Diego. I learned quickly sandals weren't allowed."

Terry Harmon "It was 1967 in Clearwater. I wore No. 54. We stayed at the Fort Harrison Hotel with all the players and staff. One of the neatest things was going to Clearwater and the drive from the airport, all the beautiful palm trees and the water and then going to work and trying to earn a position every year. All the preparation for spring training every year always led to aches and pains the first day. No matter how hard you worked at home, it wasn't the same every spring. I loved spring training. It was a time to bring your family to Clearwater for six weeks or more, spend time on the beach, and spend time with other families. I loved every minute of it. Every year I was on the ledge because I was a utility player, and someone was always trying to get my job. I was lucky enough to hang on for a few years and have a great mediocre career."

Von Hayes "My first spring training was in Tucson, Arizona, with the Cleveland Indians. I wore No. 62, and my first roommate was Chris Bando. It was my first year out of college, and I went directly to the major league camp. I was overwhelmed to say the least. The thing I remember most about my first day was how terrifying Cliff Johnson looked. While the rest of the team stretched, Cliff was on his own program, smoking cigs and generally letting everyone know how miserable he was to be in Cleveland that year. Regardless of it all, that man could hit! The best part of spring training is at the beginning when you get a chance to see your teammates again before the games start. It's a no-stress, fun time that always produces good memories. The worst part of spring training was always how long it was. I always felt that a week of practice and about 10 games was all I needed to be ready to play. I always thought the pitchers should still report in February and let the rest of the team report somewhere around the middle of March. Let them throw against a wall for a month until we got there. Just kidding, but a week less wouldn't have hurt!"

Ryan Howard "[It was] 2002 at Carpenter Complex. [I] wore a high number, something like 65 or 72. Let's see, a roommate? Either Danny Gonzalez or Chris Roberson. [I] remember going through a physical exam and then right out of the gate, a mandatory two-mile run. If you didn't do it in 16 minutes or less, you had to attend the breakfast club. That meant you had to show up every morning at 6:30 and run two miles until you met the time limit. I never made the breakfast club, fortunately. [I] went from Clearwater to Lakewood."

Ricky Jordan "It was Clearwater, 1984, training with the Spartanburg Phillies. I wore No. 6. Carpenter Field was so impressive. I had no idea that many players would be there. I always enjoyed and appreciated the hands-on instruction from the staff. I didn't like the long distance running they made us do every day or the food for lunch—soup, soup, soup."

Jim Kaat "I wore No. 21 with the original Washington Senators training in Orlando, Florida. I was nervous but proud to wear a big league uni. Coming out of Michigan, I loved the warm weather. There was only one field in those days, and I didn't like the amount of time they made us stand around in the outfield doing nothing."

John Kruk "My first big league spring training was with the San Diego Padres in beautiful Yuma, Arizona, in 1986. I was given No. 44. What I liked about spring training was getting together with the boys and having a great time on and off the field! What I disliked was everything else, meaningless games. It was way too long and boring!

My most memorable moment in my first spring was sitting in the clubhouse, but manager Dick Williams didn't show up. He decided to retire and forgot to tell the Padres."

Greg Luzinski "My first day was 1969, an invitee to spring training. I wore No. 19 from Day One. I remember being in the back room at Jack Russell Stadium with all the other rookies. I was a first baseman that first year, and Deron Johnson, the team's first baseman, took me under his wing a little, even though I was technically fighting for his job. He helped me out a lot right from the beginning. Once January came every year, you got anxious for spring training. We used to get there and spend time getting in shape. That's different today as the players are in better shape. Clearwater was a great place to bring the kids. We'd stay on the beach near other families. The kids had a better time than we did. I didn't care for road trips, especially the three-day trips. You could get more work done when you played home games compared to road games. Plus back then to go south from Clearwater you had to take Route 41. With all the traffic lights, trips took longer than today."

Charlie Manuel "[It was] 1964 with the Twins minor league camp, which was then in Fernandina Beach, Florida. [I was] told to report to Jack McKeon [one of the managers] at a hotel. [I] don't remember the name of the hotel. I can still see it but don't know the name. Jack said to check in at the front desk for a room. [I] told him I was married. He said then to check out realtors. [I] wound up with a two-bedroom apartment on the beach. I remember my first uniform number was 9. There were a lot of minor leaguers there, something like 190. I was just a kid and fit in with the rest of the young kids with talent, only I knew I could hit."

Gary Matthews "It was Casa Grande, Arizona, with the Giants minor leaguers. I wore No. 36 and had three roommates: Garry Maddox, Horace Speed, and Randy Moffitt. My fondest memory of the first day is when Willie Mays gave the outfielders a Kangaroo hide glove. This may sound strange, but I loved intrasquad games. It gave the winner bragging rights for the rest of the season. But I didn't like shagging fly balls in batting practice at all."

Tim McCarver "[It] had to be 1960 in St. Petersburg in the Cardinals minor league camp. I don't remember my uniform number other than it was under three digits. Some weren't. My roomie was Jeoff Long, a pitcher who later became a first baseman. I remember that in 1963 I was in the big league camp and I was awful. I was pressing. Heck, I missed catching some pitches by six inches. There was stress early in my career, not knowing where I would be playing that season. It seemed like you were always trying to impress someone. As an older major leaguer, there was less pressure, and you kind of developed a confident work ethic. What didn't I like? Catching. [Laughing,] it was my job. but all the catching in spring training got old. Then there was the small talk the first couple of days every spring. I remember in 1971, I came to Clearwater and passed out five business cards: 'I drove down.' 'My weight is fine.' 'I'm staying on the beach.' 'The family is fine.' "I had a nice winter.'"

Bob Miller "My first spring training was 1950 in Clearwater Athletic Field. No. 19 was hanging there for me. What a thrill it was to put on the Phillies uniform for the first time in spring training. My roommate was Curt Simmons, I believe. I remember coming out of the clubhouse for the first time, and there must have been a thousand people cheering us. I loved spring training. It was a chance to get out of the cold weather in Michigan and go to a beautiful place like Clearwater. It was always great to see the guys again. I just loved being a big league player and being a Phillie. There was nothing to dislike about spring training."

Mickey Morandini "I was with the Spartanburg club in 1990, and we trained at Carpenter Field in Clearwater. I don't remember much more than [the fact] that I survived that first day. I loved the Florida weather but didn't like the alarm clock going off at 6 AM."

Keith Moreland "My best memories were my teammates with the Phillies. Most of us were signed by the Phillies. We spent time in the minors together and came up to the big leagues together. We were part of the family with the Phillies being the parents. Going to spring training was like coming back home. Being a catcher we spent a lot of hours warming up pitchers. In the bullpen it seemed like you worked from daylight until dark. I remember saying to myself, 'We can't have any more pitchers that need to throw!'"

Ron Reed "It was 1966 with the Braves minor league camp in Waycross, Georgia. We were all housed in those ugly, old Army barracks, so the whole spring training roster were roommates. My fondest memory is that I had just finished the year playing with the Detroit Pistons in the NBA, and I thought the running the pitchers had to do was a joke. Everybody was gasping for air, and I didn't even break a sweat. I really enjoyed my years in Clearwater: golf, picking the dogs with Harry Kalas, and a lot of beach time with my girls. Waiting for the season to start was the least fond memory. I couldn't wait to head north to start playing for real."

Ray Rippelmeyer "It was 1954 in Jacksonville, Florida, training with the Toledo Triple A club in the Milwaukee Braves system. I don't remember my uniform number or my roommate. That was a long, long time ago! The first player I met was Murray Wall, who became one of my best friends in the game. He walked across the room, introduced himself, and really broke the ice. Up until then I was a little nervous. To be able to play baseball every day was a dream come true. There wasn't anything I didn't like. I loved to run, so the conditioning wasn't a problem. I had just finished playing a full season of college basketball, so I was in good running shape. I just had to get my arm in shape. I started my coaching career with the Phillies in 1966 as their Triple A pitching coach in San Diego, and we trained in Dunedin."

Mike Rogodzinski "March 1970 was my first spring training. My uniform was made of heavy wool with chips of wood sewn in for durability. I don't remember the number, but it was three digits. I came out of college thinking I might play at the Class A level. But Andy Seminick gave me a chance to work out with his Double A team that first day. Boy, was I lucky. I roomed with a left-handed pitcher from the state of Washington named Tom Horne. What I don't miss is lunch. The coaches would walk around with sandwiches while us grunts got a Dixie cup of the day's soup with two packs of crackers. We also were given a cup of Gatorade to wash it all down. Talk about living large."

Jimmy Rollins "[It was] 1997 at Carpenter Complex. My number was 63 or 68. I remember we stayed at the EconoLodge down the street from the complex, but I can't remember my roommate. [I] didn't expect to see that many players in the clubhouse, something like 200 of us. It was like going to school the first day. You had to find your locker and you had to learn new names and faces. Yet everybody knew everything about you, where you came from, what round you were selected."

Juan Samuel "[It was] 1981 in the Phillies minor league camp at the Complex. [I] stayed at the Days Inn in Pinellas Park. My first roommate was Juan Nataniel, but he got released. Then Julio Espinosa, Nino's brother. That was my first flight and first time out of the Dominican. I remember wearing a three-piece, light blue, pinstriped suit. The shuttle ride from the Tampa airport was an adventure. I told the driver we were staying at the Days Inn on Clearwater Beach, but we couldn't find it. Finally, he asked to see my information sheet from the Phillies. The hotel was in Pinellas Park and not on the beach."

Ryne Sandberg "[It was] 1979 at Carpenter Complex. We stayed at the Days Inn up on 19. [My] roommate was Ray Borucki first and then Ed Hearn. A bus took us from the hotel to Carpenter. As the bus drove in the driveway at the complex on the first day, Pete Rose was in the batting cages. When I got off the bus, I stopped and just watched him hit. All I saw were line drives. I was thinking, *Wow, that's Pete Rose.*"

Kevin Sefcik "My favorite thing about spring training had to be the weather. Coming down from Chicago in mid-February was awesome. Clearwater is a great location. I experienced a couple of other areas in spring training after leaving the Phillies, and nothing was better than Clearwater. My least favorite part? Nothing. There is nothing better than playing baseball—whether it was spring training or the season."

Mike Schmidt "My first minor league camp was in 1972 at Carpenter Complex. Remembering my number or roommate? I have no idea. I do remember that we stayed at the old West Coast Hotel in downtown Clearwater. The following spring I was in the big league camp at Jack Russell, and my number was 22. What I most remember about the first day? The circle jerk and all those other archaic physical fitness regiments they put us through. At the end of the camp, I was sent all the way to the opposite end of the country, Eugene, Oregon, then the Phillies' Triple A team."

Rich Schu "It was 1981 in the Phillies minor league camp in Clearwater. Dean Baugh was my roommate. I remember putting on the Phillies uniform for the first time and what a thrill that was. I also remember seeing 160 guys searching for the same dream of making it to the majors. Three years later was my first camp with the big club. [I was] No. 53. My two roommates were Kenny Dowell and Tony Ghelfi. It was a thrill to be in the same clubhouse as my idols such as Mike Schmidt. I always enjoyed seeing my teammates every spring training. I remember playing in those B games right out of bed early in the morning and then having to wait all day to play a couple of innings late in the main spring training games. There was a lot of stress, trying to make the big club out of spring training."

Don Seger "My first spring training was 1955 in Winston-Salem, North Carolina, as a trainer for the Quincy Gems of the Three-I League. My roommate was the manager, Vern Hoscheit. After driving through a snowstorm for nearly two days, the warm weather in North Carolina was most welcome. I always liked seeing the old players again and meeting the new ones, especially the wide-eyed rookies. I found it difficult to find something to dislike, being that we were in good weather at that time of the year. During my first year in the Yankees major league camp, we had Leroy [Lee] Thomas and Tony Kubek, which made it memorable."

Kevin Stocker "I remember being so excited and nervous in spring training. Strangers became good teammates and friends. Once I was cut but brought back to the big club for a game in St. Petersburg in 1993.

Hollins got hit by a pitch, charged the mound, and before I knew what was going on, I was the only person on the bench. It was the first of four brawls that year. Needless to say, that was a tough team. I'm from the Northwest where we were stuck inside all winter working out. Getting to Clearwater with the warm weather and grass and finally getting to work out outside was the best part. For me it was a treat. I know it is big business, but the length of spring training was ridiculous. It would be nice if it could be shortened a little. That's my opinion. At the same time, I can see both sides."

Kent Tekulve "It was 1970 with the Pirates in Bradenton, Florida. I don't remember the uniform number. I was just so happy to have one. Bruce Kison was my roomie. Winter was over, and we got to play baseball again, and for me personally, it was warm in February compared to home. I signed in the middle of '69, so it was great to see my teammates the following spring. I got to do what I liked best—throw a baseball. I had no dislikes about spring training. It was paradise."

Del Unser "It was Lake Wales, Florida, in 1967, the minor league camp of the Washington Senators. I remember it well because I had an appendectomy after two days and missed the rest of spring. June Raines was my roomie and he helped me get to the hospital. My fondest memory was going to the local pub and getting to know some of my new minor league teammates. During my rookie big league camp, I was assigned No. 30. The best part of that camp was making the big club and getting to see my wife in Louisville, Kentucky, before the last spring exhibition game."

Chase Utley "I signed in 2000 and went right to Batavia. So my first spring camp was the following year, and I was invited to the major league camp, which was at Jack Russell Stadium. My number was 80. A bunch of lockers were in the middle of the room, and that's where I was along with the other rookies. [I] stayed at the EconoLodge but didn't have a roommate, which was fine. I was among those in the first cut. When I walked in the clubhouse there were so many of the players I had watched on TV four to five months ago. It was a very cool experience."

Eric Valent "My first year of major league camp was 2001. Number 71. I had a locker on the 'island' in the middle of the Jack Russell Stadium clubhouse. Nick Punto and Johnny Estrada were my roommates. Our first big league camp, we knew we were going to [Triple A] Scranton, but it was great being in the big camp because it meant we didn't have to spend as much time in the minor league camp. Everybody worked toward their goals for the upcoming season. It was a clean start for everyone and a fresh start to the new season. There's nothing I didn't enjoy about my spring trainings. The early morning wake-up calls didn't bother me nor did the extra work in the weight room or batting cages. That's what you were there for. One needs to put forth the effort in all aspects to become the best player they can be. One's career is short-lived, so it's imperative to be focused and determined each and every day."

Shane Victorino "[In] 2000 as a 19-year-old kid from Hawaii in the fabled Dodgertown over in Vero Beach. It was my first time away from home. I had always heard about Dodgertown. All of the players were there, minor leaguers and big leaguers. We stayed in a dorm, four per room. We all ate in a big dining room along with such stars as Koufax, Wills. I thought this was the best thing ever. [I] had so much fun. [I] couldn't believe I was in the same place and playing on the same fields as Jackie Robinson and all the greats."

Ozzie Virgil "I was in the Phillies minor league camp in 1977. I remember that I wore No. 44, but I didn't have a roommate. Lucky me. What impressed me was how good every player was in camp. I enjoyed being in Florida and working to become a better player. The hardest part was seeing your friends get released and sent home."

Mitch Williams "I was 19 years old and had been taken by the Rangers in the Rule 5 draft. It was my first big league camp. I was walking out early in the morning and I remember the Rangers had just gotten Cliff Johnson. Cliff was standing in right field, and Mickey Rivers was sitting on the ground. I walked toward them, and Mickey [made fun of me, saying], 'Clifford, look at the head on this critter.' I later learned that Mickey was one of the many real characters during my career. It was always great to reunite with your teammates every spring. I also remember all the aches and pains that came every year no matter how much winter ball you had played or how hard you had worked. The best part of spring training, though, was the end."

Opening Day

Regardless of where we had finished the previous season, there was always hope on Opening Day. After all, everybody was 0–0. Fans were always juiced for the openers. Baseball was back, and winter blues were finally gone. Giles grew up in Cincinnati where the season opener was like a holiday. Schools closed; many fans took off from work. It was a very festive occasion. That didn't exist in Philadelphia, but Giles decided to change that. Enter Kiteman and many other crazy promotions, which were designed to make Opening Day special, something fans wouldn't forget. Giles loved to come up with an Opening Day act, and we had plenty.

I remember Schmidt delivering a dramatic game-winning homer off the Mets' Tug McGraw in 1974. In 1982 the home opener, which was also the season opener, was postponed by snow. It was the first season in which David Montgomery was the executive vice president and responsible for weather-related, game-time decisions. We were at the Vet early in the morning for some live TV interviews, announcing the game was postponed by snow and cold weather.

Opening Day Memories

Marty Bystrom "Seeing 'Irish' Mike Ryan catch a ball dropped from a helicopter. [I] still don't know how he did it."

Steve Carlton "Losing to Tom Seaver at Shea Stadium in a game that took 1 hour, 56 minutes."

Larry Christenson "April 6, 1973, at Shea Stadium in New York, Steve Carlton vs. Tom Seaver. I was 19 years old and the youngest player in the majors. Willie Mays was in the Mets dugout as a player and at the end of a great career. Seaver struck out eight and beat Carlton in a very close game. I was on the front step as close to home plate as possible and remember the explosive fastballs from each of them. I was scheduled to pitch in Game 3 against Koosman but got rained out. They held me back until a game against the Mets on Friday, April 13. I won my debut, pitching a complete game."

Jim Eisenreich "My first Opening Day was 1982 with the Twins in the first regular season game ever played in the Metrodome. Some 30-plus family members and friends were there. I grew up an hour north of Minneapolis, so it was a very special day in many ways, even though I was hitless in three at-bats."

Terry Francona "While with the Reds, hitting a home run in 1987 off Floyd Youmans of the Expos, my former team."

Jim Fregosi "Hitting a home run on Opening Day off Seattle's Marty Pattin."

Dallas Green "There are two special memories: my first opener as the Phillies manager in 1980 and then receiving our World Series rings the following year."

Tommy Greene "Being in the bullpen in San Francisco. All the relievers were cramped in the little box in left field. [It] reminded me of a chicken coop."

Terry Harmon "Getting a hit in my very first at-bat in the major leagues. That was quite a thrill."

Dave Hollins "I was pinch-hitting against the Cubs and hit a scorcher up the middle that looked like a sure hit, but [Ryne] Sandberg made an unbelievable diving stop and nailed me at first base."

Ricky Jordan "Being in the starting lineup for the 1989 opener at the Vet and hearing the loud cheers for me."

Jim Kaat "Seeing President Eisenhower throw out the ceremonial first ball...He threw it from his box into a crowd of us, and coach Clyde McCullough caught it. That's one great memory. Another was in 1965 when I had to be helicoptered into Met Stadium in Bloomington because of floods in the area. [I] wound up pitching nine innings against the Yankees, a game we won in 11 innings 5–4.

Frank Lucchesi "Well, I have two great memories from Opening Day, and both were with the Phillies. 1970 at Connie Mack Stadium, after 21 years in the minor leagues, I was finally in the major leagues as a manager. Very emotional day. Then 1971, the first game ever played in Veterans Stadium. Both hold very special places in my heart."

Greg Luzinski "1972, a nervous rookie in Chicago in front of my family. [I] hit a home run off Fergie Jenkins, and we won 4–2."

Tim McCarver "My very first opening day with the Cardinals was not a fond memory...I was on the bench."

Mickey Morandini "[It] has to be Mike Ryan catching a ball dropped from a helicopter at the Vet."

Bruce Ruffin "Being there for the first Opening Day in Coors Field."

Dick Ruthven "As a nervous rookie, throwing strikes on my first two pitches is something I remember the most."

Ryne Sandberg "I made the Cubs' Opening Day lineup at third base in Cincinnati. Going to home plate and seeing Johnny Bench behind the plate was a thrill."

Mike Schmidt "First game of the 1974 season, I hit a game-winning, two-run home run with one out in the last of the ninth inning to beat the Mets and Tug McGraw 5–4. Later, Tug became a teammate and a very good friend. We shared a lot of rides to the Vet from our suburban Philly homes."

Kevin Stocker "Opening in Colorado in a snowstorm, wearing two pair of batting gloves for warmth. Perhaps not my fondest but certainly the most memorable."

Kent Tekulve "The size of the crowd, the excitement, and optimistic attitude about what the season could bring."

Del Unser "[It] has to be my first hit, a line-drive single to left in my second at-bat."

CHAPTER 11
ALL-STAR GAMES

Major League Baseball's jewel events are All-Star Games and postseason games, especially the World Series. The Phillies were "jewel-less" for many years. It all began to change as the mid-1970s came along. Though not a "jewel" event, we hosted our first ABC Monday night telecast on July 5, 1976. A certain excitement gripped the city. After all, the great Howard Cosell was coming to the Vet. I thought I should introduce myself—not that he cared—to see if he needed anything, thinking he might want a media guide or something along those lines. He paused before saying, "Yes, son. Can you get me a bottle of vodka?" It was not what I was expecting, but I did deliver. Eight days later we got our first real chance to shine as we hosted the All-Star Game, the first in Philadelphia since 1952.

The host club's public relations staff was responsible for everything involving the media plus printing the program. That was the same season in which we started winning. So, there was no drag time. The game was a great dress rehearsal for postseason media accommodations, something we would experience that fall. The Vet was a good facility when it came to camera locations, TV requirements, media needs, hospitality functions, etc. All media seating was on the 300 level, baseball press box, football press box, and stadium club.

The Bellevue Hotel was the All-Star Game headquarters hotel. We had a large suite, which served as the room for distribution of the credentials. Today, Major League Baseball screens all credential requests for jewel events, but back then I had declined someone who had applied. I don't remember his name or affiliation or the circumstances. Somehow, this guy got a credential, and I had him tossed—not once but twice.

Word came that President Ford was going to attend the game. The Secret Service profiled all of us. I was given a certain pin to wear that meant I had total access. The president arrived at the Phillies executive office entrance, took the elevator to the office floor that included the PR office, and walked down the hall to Bill Giles' office. I was in the PR office at the time. When the president arrived, I was informed not to leave my office until he had passed by. So, I never met or saw him.

Since it was the city's bicentennial, Giles wanted to showcase not only the ballclub but the city of Philadelphia. He was a huge advocate of promoting the city and very active in the community. He wanted to have a large gala party the night before the game. We went to the naval yard and toured some of the old battleships. He thought it would make a terrific setting for the party. Later he learned there were military regulations against having booze on ships, so that idea went into mothballs. He finally organized the party in a huge tent near the Liberty Bell. It turned into a tradition for the midsummer game. Giles was the pioneer.

Starting with this game, "O Canada" and "The Star-Spangled Banner" would be sung on an annual basis. Due to some ballot stuffing, the Cincinnati Reds had five players in the National League's starting lineup. On the bench the Big Red Machine had two more players. Led by the game's MVP, Reds outfielder George Foster, the National League coasted to a 7–1 win before 63,974, the third largest crowd in the game's history. The Reds players combined for seven hits, four runs scored, and four RBI.

Our fans had plenty to cheer about as we had five players on the NL squad, the most in our history—Greg Luzinski, who started in left field and reserves Bob Boone, Dave Cash, Larry Bowa, and Mike Schmidt. Manager Danny Ozark was a coach. Needless to say, they drew the loudest pre-game cheers and when they came to bat. There was plenty of other Phillies flavor that night as numerous alumni were involved—Robin Roberts (NL honorary captain), Sparky Anderson (NL manager), Gene Mauch (AL coach), Woodie Fryman and Dick Ruthven (NL pitchers), Don Money (AL reserve), and Bob Uecker (ABC broadcaster). It certainly was a night for Phillies fans to cherish.

As the site of the Continental Congress and the signing of the Declaration of Independence, Philadelphia, in addition to this All-Star Game, hosted the NBA and NHL All-Star Games and the NCAA Final Four. It was a grand slam for the city.

Twenty years later baseball's All-Star classic returned to Veterans Stadium. MLB had assumed more control of the festivities and media aspects, which made it a little easier to endure. Giles' party took place at Penn's Landing, another showcase location for the city. This time we had only one representative on the NL team, reliever Ricky Bottalico. The game was a no-contest 6–0 win for the National League. It was a historic win, to some extent as the

Philadelphia fans received another chance to cheer Steve Carlton—their star pitcher seen here years before, acknowledging an ovation from Veterans Stadium fans—during the 1996 All-Star Game.

NL didn't win another game until 2010. Philadelphia area native Mike Piazza walked off with the MVP Award. Future Hall of Famer Ozzie Smith made his 15th and last ASG appearance, drawing a standing ovation when he entered the game in the sixth inning.

The biggest cheer, however, occurred when four Phillies Hall of Famers—Steve Carlton, Schmidt, Richie Ashburn, and congressman Jim Bunning—participated in the ceremonial first pitch. The loudest boos were reserved for Toronto Blue Jays outfielder Joe Carter, who heard it before his name was ever introduced. Phillies fans hadn't forgotten his World Series-ending home run three years earlier.

The biggest difference between the two All-Star Games was the additional festivities in 1996. A five-day All-Star Fanfest of over 25 exhibits was held at the Philadelphia Convention Center, and Monday was the All-Star Workout Day that included a celebrity softball game, workouts by both squads, and the Gillette Home Run Derby.

ALL-STAR GAME MEMORIES

Larry Andersen "Fondest All-Star Game memory? Easy spending the three days off in Ocean City, New Jersey."

Bob Boone "1976 game in Philly, my first. [I] will never forget the ovation that the Philly fans gave us during the pregame introductions. I still get emotional when I think about it."

Larry Bowa "[I] was on five All-Star teams, but playing in Philly in 1976 without a doubt is my greatest memory. The crowd was awesome, and the infield was Schmidt, me, and Dave Cash. [It was a] great feeling playing at the Vet in front of your home crowd."

Dave Cash "Sitting on the bench at the Vet in 1976 next to Tony Perez while Steve Garvey [first base] and Joe Morgan [second base] started at our positions. Sparky Anderson was the manager, and Tony kept pestering him, 'Sparky, when are you going to let Dave and me play?' I did eventually get in the game, singled, and scored."

Darren Daulton "Sitting in the dugout during the celebrity game with Michael Jordan and Bob Costas at Camden Yards [in 1993]. Jordan just hit and didn't drive in the runners on base. When he came back to the dugout, I told him he needs to keep his day job. Costas started laughing, and Jordan said, 'Are you kidding me? You and Joe Carter haven't driven in a run in nine games.'"

David Doster "I got called up to the Phillies in 1996 right before the All-Star Game. [My wife] Kim, [son] Owen, Kim's brother, and I went to the festivities, including the Home Run Derby and game. We were on the lower level concourse for the Home Run Derby and couldn't see Mark McGwire's home runs landed in the upper deck. We had a blast. The next week I was back at the Vet playing on the same field as those All-Stars."

Jim Fregosi "I actually have two fond memories. I led off the game in Houston [in 1968] with a double against Don Drysdale. The second, managing the 1994 NL team to a win in Three Rivers Stadium."

Kevin Gross "My best memory is being selected to the 1988 All-Star team along with my great teammate and friend, Lance Parrish. I pitched one inning [in Riverfront Stadium] and faced three great players Dave Winfield, Cal Ripken, and Jose Canseco, retiring them in order. What a great memory. I will always cherish being part of baseball's best in 1988."

Von Hayes "Getting a base hit and driving in a run in my only at-bat. Afterward getting calls from all my friends telling me they were interviewing a pitcher on the American League team during the game [in Anaheim], and they didn't show my hit. Oh, well, I still have a 1.000 average as an All-Star."

Al Holland "I would have to say that my fondest memory would be when I was selected to the 1984 All-Star team with the Phillies. Although I did not get to pitch in the game, being selected was a great honor. The game was played at Candlestick Park, home of the San Francisco Giants, my former team. It was an absolute thrill to be a teammate with so many great ballplayers, even if only for one day."

Jim Kaat "Facing Willie Mays, Roberto Clemente, Hank Aaron, Willie McCovey, Dick Allen, Ron Santo, and Joe Torre in 1966...on a 110-degree day in St. Louis."

John Kruk "Striking out twice in three at-bats in Camden Yards [in 1993]. Everybody remembers one of them against Randy Johnson. I didn't have a chance. All I wanted to do is escape with my life."

Mike Lieberthal "The first year it was so exciting to be among the best players in the game. [I] batted once and was hitless. The next year, I got a hit off Mariano Rivera and scored. Can't beat that for a great memory."

Greg Luzinski "My first at-bat in Yankee Stadium came in an All-Star Game [in 1977], and I hit a two-run homer to right field off Jim Palmer."

Art Mahaffey "First of all it was such a great honor to be picked to play in an All-Star Game. The players voted for you back in those days, so it was all the players in the National League that voted and picked me, Sandy Koufax, Don Drysdale, Warren Spahn, and five other pitchers in 1961. Imagine the thrill to be picked along with those names. Bob Gibson and Juan Marichal were not picked. I pitched two hitless innings in Fenway Park in the second game in 1961 and faced Norm Cash, Rocky Colavito, Al Kaline, Mickey Mantle, Roger Maris, Luis Aparicio, and Johnny Temple."

Tim McCarver "Scoring the winning run in the 1966 game that was played in St. Louis [is] something I'll always remember."

Juan Samuel "As a rookie in 1984, I was selected for the game that was played in San Francisco. There were eight other All-Stars from the Dominican Republic, so we had a 'team photo' taken. I still have that photo in my home. The manager was Paul Owens, and my manager didn't get me in the game [laughing]. After the game the spread included a big pile of Dungeness crabs. Since I didn't get to play in the game, that was my fondest memory—pigging out on crabs."

Ryne Sandberg "Getting to start in my first All-Star Game in 1984. I wanted to be an All-Star every year."

Curt Schilling "Telling Alex Rodriguez in batting practice the day before the 2002 game that when he hit in the game, I was going to throw him nothing but my best fastball [and] then doing it."

Mike Schmidt "[My] game-winning home run in 1981 off Rollie Fingers, a two-run shot over the center-field fence at Cleveland Stadium in the top of the eighth, a 5–4 win for our manager, Dallas Green."

Bobby Shantz "[The] 1952 game at Shibe Park and striking out Whitey Lockman, Jackie Robinson, and Stan Musial in the fifth inning."

Curt Simmons "I was in three games and started two, 1952 and 1957. For some reason I was late getting to the park [in 1952]. Leo Durocher was the manager [and said], 'Curt, we're going over the hitters. Robbie [Roberts] pitched two days ago, so you're starting.' I pitched three scoreless innings. In 1957 I started in St. Louis against Jim Bunning. I got through the first inning but walked Ted Williams and Yogi Berra to start the second inning. Walter Alston came to the mound and took me out."

Tony Taylor "Being able to participate in the game with all the best players, especially the Latin American stars. We all share our memories."

Rick Wise "My first game in the old Tiger Stadium, I sat in the bullpen the whole game but got a great view of Reggie Jackson's home run into the light tower in right field."

CHAPTER 12
UNFULFILLED CHAMPIONSHIP SEASONS

During my career the Phillies have had their share of peaks and valleys. They almost reached the World Series in 1964, my rookie season, and then they had a string of down years, including 1969 when the Phillies almost lost 100 games. They lost 99 games in '69, something I never experienced again. But through the draft that started in 1965, they began building a farm system that would produce the nucleus that would lead to the best era in the history of the franchise, an era that was finally surpassed starting in 2007.

I'll never forget our 1975 caravan stop in Allentown, Pennsylvania. Third-year manager Danny Ozark told the audience, "We're building a dynasty." I shuddered. We finished the previous season 80–82. Well, Ozark was right. We won 86 games in 1975 and then were National League East champions for three straight years. Starting in 1976, the Phillies recorded 101, 101, and 90-win seasons.

1976

The ghost of 1964 showed up again in 1976. Leading by 15½ games on August 24, we spiraled downward, losing 17 of 23 games, including eight in a row. Before we knew it, that big lead was down to three games on September 17. Six wins later we were on the brink of wiping away another 1964 finish. We had a chance to clinch during a five-game series in Montreal. Chris Wheeler, my public relations colleague, was on that road trip, but I decided my wife, Julie, and I, were going to be there to share in the glory after years of suffering. We flew to Montreal with Marcelle Owens, Paul's wife.

It was a cold, damp Sunday afternoon in old Jarry Parc, but the excitement of clinching the division overrode the weather. We had a doubleheader against the Expos, managed by my old friend Gene Mauch. We won the first game to clinch, setting off a champagne party in the clubhouse. In the fifth inning of the second game, Wheeler walked into the booth. Richie Ashburn left, saying, "You always wanted to give this a try, so go ahead." That, my friends, was the start of a long broadcasting career for Wheeler.

NLCS

A young, homegrown team proved no match for the Big Red Machine from Cincinnati. We led in all three games, including 6–4, going into the end of the ninth inning in Cincinnati in Game 3. The Reds came up with three runs in their last at-bat, completing a sweep of the NL Championship Series. Sparky Anderson's club then swept the New York Yankees in four games to win the world championship. It almost seemed as if we were glad to win the division and were no match for a hot team. Chalk it up as a terrific learning experience.

One number stood out from that season—11. That was the number of pitchers we used for the entire 162-game season, the fewest in club history. That record may never be broken. The All-Star Game in 1976 was our first jewel event, but we failed to get to the really big jewel, World Series, that same year.

1977

M any considered the 1977 club our best team of the era, especially when Bake McBride was acquired in a midseason trade. He hit .339 in 85 games with his new team. Ozark's bench included Davey Johnson, Ollie Brown, and Jerry Martin from the right side and Jay Johnstone and Tim McCarver from left side. Starters Steve Carlton, Larry Christenson, Randy Lerch, Jim Lonborg, and Jim Kaat combined for 69 wins. The bullpen of Tug McGraw, Ron Reed, Gene Garber, and Warren Brusstar had 29 wins and 46 saves. Greg Luzinski had a monster year and finished second in the NL MVP race. Carlton won his second Cy Young.

But it wasn't an easy ride to their second consecutive 101-win season. On June 29 a 39–32 record had the Phillies eight and a half games out of first place. Between August 3 and 23, we went 19–1, including a club-record 13-game winning streak to take a seven and half game lead. It ended with a 15–9 romp in Chicago, Game No. 157 on September 27 with Christenson starting, winning, and hitting a home run.

NLCS

This time the Los Angeles Dodgers stood in our way of a trip to the World Series during a best-of-five NLCS. A split of two games in Los Angeles sent the series to the Vet where we had a great home-field advantage, posting a 60–21 record. Game 3 turned out to be a game like no other in our history. Dodgers starter Burt Hooton began to struggle with his control in the second inning, sending the Vet crowd into a tizzy I have never experienced. With each ball out of the strike zone, the crowd got louder and louder. A crowd of 63,719 literally hooted Hooton out of the game that inning when he walked three consecutive batters, forcing in three runs to give us a 3–2 lead.

Two more runs in the eighth seemed to give the Phillies a commanding lead. All we needed was three more outs. But all the glee turned sour in just five batters in the top of the ninth. Gene Garber was in his third inning of relief. He had retired eight straight Dodgers on ground-outs and was one out away from a save. Pinch-hitter Vic Davalillo laid down a bunt for a base hit, and pinch-hitter Manny Mota hit an 0–2 pitch to left field. Luzinski went back to the fence, leapt, and had the ball in his glove but couldn't hold it. The relay throw got away, putting Mota on third with the tying run. Davey Lopes hit a hot smash to third. The ball went off Mike Schmidt's glove, but the always alert Larry Bowa grabbed it bare-handed and fired to first for an apparent game-ending out. Umpire Bruce Froemming called Lopes safe. An errant pick-off throw from Garber moved Lopes to second from where he scored the winning run on a Bill Russell grounder up the middle.

The game will be forever remembered in our history as Black Friday. The bitter loss sucked the life out of us. Playing in a steady rain the next night, the Dodgers advanced to the series. Rain or shine, it didn't matter. Black Friday had unofficially ended the season. "My fondest postseason memory was a game that also turned into my greatest nightmare," Garber said. TV replays showed Lopes was out, but Froemming had the call. To his credit Garber was classy, never pointing a finger at Froemming. Everyone else in Philadelphia certainly did.

1978

Unlike the previous two seasons, we led the NL East for the bulk of the season—131 days to be precise. Two key midseason trades brought starter Dick Ruthven back to the Phillies and Rawly Eastwick to the pen. A June 23 doubleheader sweep of the Chicago Cubs at the Vet put us in first place, and we never looked back. The biggest deficit was three and a half games; the biggest pad was five and a half.

Even though we led most of the way, we finished 11 games behind where we did the previous two seasons. The clinching game was the second-to-last game, a September 30 contest in Pittsburgh. Winner Randy Lerch went only five innings, but he homered in his two at-bats, which paved the way for a 10–8, division-clinching decision. Ron Reed struck out Willie Stargell and got Phil Garner on a grounder to end the game. Each represented the tying run. It was the fourth straight year the Phillies and Pirates battled for supremacy in the division.

NLCS

Once again we met the Dodgers in the best-of-five NLCS. Los Angeles won both games at the Vet, leaving Phillies fans in a sour mood and left to their favorite way of expressing themselves—booing. Carlton almost single-handedly saved us from a quick exit with a complete-game, 9–4 win in Dodger Stadium. Lefty also homered and drove in four runs. Postgame interview rooms are set up for the media mass in the postseason, but Carlton didn't talk to the media. I somehow had to get him to the interview room.

As soon as the game ended and Carlton got to our first-base dugout, I grabbed him by the belt. He asked, "Where are we going?" I mumbled, "the interview room." The room was located behind the Dodgers third-base dugout. The only way to get there was to walk across the field, into their dugout, past their clubhouse, and into a room crowded with media. He stood at the podium and answered a few questions, using a whispering voice. Finding our way back to our clubhouse seemed like an eternity. I didn't say anything, and he didn't complain.

In all the years that Carlton was in the postseason with us, that's the only time I really needed him for the interview room. During the other times, there were other stars I could take—often McGraw. Russell, who delivered the crushing hit on Black Friday, did it again the next day, a 10th-inning single off McGraw after Garry Maddox had dropped a potential third out.

Major League Baseball rules state clubhouses are to open immediately after the last out of a clinching game. But how could I open the clubhouse after seeing McGraw with his head in his hands, crying, and Maddux sitting quietly facing his locker? They and the rest of the players deserved some time to themselves before facing the media horde. I delayed the opening of the locker room, but the media did not complain. After that we traveled home. The flight from Los Angeles to Philadelphia is always a long one, but that one seemed to take forever.

1979

After three straight seasons of falling short, we signed free agent Pete Rose to the richest contract ever, $3.2 million, after the 1978 season. He was the proven winner and leader we were missing. With the addition of Rose and Manny Trillo, we were strong favorites to win our fourth straight NL East title.

When we acquired Trillo from the Cubs, Paul Owens was in Florida. Wheeler and I were driving to spring training separately. We had the same routine, staying one night at a Holiday Inn in Santee, South Carolina. I was about to call it a night, but the hotel phone rang. "Baron did you see the TV? We just got Trillo in a trade," Wheeler said. "Do you know anything about it?" I had no idea. We both wondered if we held a press conference in Philly, but Owens wasn't there, and neither were we. How was the trade announced in the pre-cell phone era? Next day we learned the trade was announced by Dallas Green, director of minor leagues and scouting, and Adele Mizia, the PR department's highly efficient secretary.

Injuries dominated our press releases that season, a constant string that prohibited the club from getting any momentum started. Rose was the only regular position starter who didn't miss a game because of injuries. The starting eight started just 74 games. "Injuries are part of any sport," Owens said. "But I never remember a club getting so many key injuries. I'll never forget our July 4th press release, the fact Ruthven and Christenson were going on the DL, and Lerch broke his wrist. From a five-man rotation, we went to two in 24 hours."

From the preseason favorites, we fell to fourth. This club was getting up there in age, too. After another August loss that year, Wheeler, Dennis Lehman, and I were sitting in our office at the Vet, bemoaning what was happening. All of a sudden we heard a blaring voice, saying, "Hey, let's go." It was Green. Lehman said, "Dallas, we need you to manage this team." He responded, "Are you crazy? I'm not going down there." Weeks later he replaced Ozark.

2007

As the years continued to march on, I sat down with David Montgomery in 2006 and felt it was time for someone else to head the department. So 2007 was the last season under my full-time watch. Fortunately, the club was very interested in letting me step into a part-time role in alumni relations, a perfect fit. I was the honoree on alumni night that August. Instead of writing the script, I was the script on the field. My family knew about the honor, but I didn't. Well, I'd been around long enough to know how we operate. Then the next day, I had a big party with alumni, friends, and family. The press box at Citizens Bank Park was named "Baron's Box." It was a very humble honor indeed. With Pat Gillick in his second year as the general manager and a new bunch of young, homegrown players, we won the NL East title at home, the first championship in our three-year-old park.

NLCS

Mirroring 1976 the young club lost three straight to a red hot Colorado Rockies team. It was another tough learning experience. Like all losing clubhouse scenes in the postseason, ours was very quiet. Charlie Manuel

177

had to go to the interview room after we lost. At Coors Field, it meant walking down the left-field line to a tent set up outside the ballpark. The Rockies, however, did provide a golf cart. As you walk around the clubhouse, there's not much to say to your players. Aaron Rowand, a pending free agent, and I made eye contact. He reached out and gave me a huge hug—well, a crushing hug, actually—as he's very strong. Nothing was said, but we both knew our careers with the Phillies were about to end.

CHAPTER 13
WORLD SERIES SEASONS

1980

The question was whether this club would win it all or whether Paul Owens should break it up. With Dallas Green in the dugout, Owens wanted to give the club one more chance. It certainly wasn't a picnic. Green screamed and yelled at players, benched veterans, and played rookies like Lonnie Smith and Keith Moreland. Another rookie, Bob Walk, was in the rotation. Come September, Marty Bystrom was plugged into the rotation and went 5–0 the final month.

Bouncing around between second and third place, the Phillies finally grabbed the lead on July 11. It lasted two days. In early August they lost a four-game series to the Pirates in Pittsburgh to fall a season-worst six games behind. Green had a classic airing out session between games of a double-header loss. Media waited outside the clubhouse to gain access, but they were treated with Green's tirade. His voice can carry through cement.

The club responded by going 13–6 before losing the last two games of the month in San Diego. Owens couldn't take anymore of the lackadaisical play. Before a September 1 day game in San Francisco, he called a clubhouse meeting and unloaded a profanity-filled outburst, challenging players. Four straight wins followed, putting them on top again.

With the second-place Montreal Expos in town for the last home weekend series, we won on Friday and lost the next two, dropping to second. Then the most pivotal game of the season happened. On a Monday night before a small crowd of 21,000, the Phillies fell behind 5–3 when the Chicago Cubs scored twice in the top of the 15th inning. The few fans who were still there had turned nasty. We rallied to win 6–5 by scoring three runs in our 15th with Manny Trillo getting the dramatic game-winning hit, the start of a six-game winning streak at the most critical time of the pennant race.

Tied with the Expos, Philadelphia went to Montreal for the final three games. Mike Schmidt, who was often criticized for not hitting in the clutch, drove in both runs of a 2–1 win. Then he followed with a two-run, game-winning homer the next day to clinch the National League East. Andy Musser, broadcasting on radio, had his greatest call, saying, "He buried it." In extra-inning games the final month, we were now 7–1. Those pressure-packed games primed us for what was to follow.

Greatest NLCS Series Ever

The National League Championship Series against Houston will be remembered as the most gut-wrenching series ever. The last four games of the five-game series went extra innings with the Phillies winning the last two in the deafening Astrodome. Down two games to one, a fourth failure at advancing to the World Series in the last five years appeared to be inevitable. Down 2–0 after seven innings in Game 4, the Phillies scored three to take a 3–2 lead only to see Houston tie it in the bottom of the ninth. Two runs in the 10th produced a 5–3 win that sent both clubs to a decisive Game 5 on October 12.

My wife, Julie, stayed in Houston while I went home after that game. I needed to get ready for a possible World Series that would start on October 14. Boxes of media credentials, parking passes, hospitality cards, information cards, World Series press pins, and credentials for other club executives were stacked in the Vet public relations office.

Front office employees were in the press dining room watching Game 5. While Julie got doused by beer from some unruly Astros fans, I was enjoying a cold brew as I needed something to calm the nerves. After a while I went to my office where I paced the floor and watched on a small television. With the Phillies trailing 5–2 to Nolan Ryan after seven innings, I got some big trash containers and was preparing to dump the boxes of credentials. We scored five in the eighth to take a lead, and it was back to preparing those passes, cards, and other materials. Houston tied the game in the last of the eighth, and I was ready to trash everything again. When Maddox caught the last out and we were headed for the World Series, out came the boxes, joyously. Julie was celebrating with the players' wives. I was celebrating with fellow employees. Finally, a World Series!

I checked in at the Franklin Plaza Hotel well after midnight. We were the first event in the new hotel. As a bellman was unloading my boxes in my suite, workers were bringing in two table lamps. There was no time for sleep, no time to enjoy the euphoria—just time to work. One of the public relations directors that came to help during the series was my friend, Bob Brown, of the Baltimore Orioles. I had visited "Brownie" in the mid-1970s to pick his brain on postseason experiences. He had been through many with the Orioles. I remember him saying, "When you get to Game 7 of the World Series, you're so worn out you don't care who wins."

Brown was assigned to help distribute credentials at the hotel. I had to leave for a few hours that evening. When I returned to my room, I discovered I had been invaded by black and orange Orioles decals. They were everywhere: on the bathroom mirror, on the toilet seat, on the shower walls, in the dresser drawers, on the TV, under the pillows, and on the brand new lamps.

One of the most time-consuming parts of preparing for a jewel event was screening credential requests. Foreign media were the most difficult. All of a sudden, three persons from a different country would show up seeking media credentials. There was no way to verify their authenticity. Basically, they were given only a seat but not access to the field, clubhouse, or interview room.

Clubhouse credentials were limited. Clubhouses simply couldn't hold the volume of media. A special sticker was placed on credentials that allowed clubhouse access. Writers complained because they didn't receive access. I had to carry extra stickers to accommodate some of the complainers. Assigning press box seats was time-consuming. Currently there's a system for assigning seats, but there wasn't one back in 1980. Philly writers urged New York writers be assigned seats in the far reaches from the main press box because they were treated that way during the World Series in New York in the 1970s. We couldn't let that happen.

The Baseball Writers Association of America had control of the press boxes for years. I got into a big argument in 1980 with the top executives of the BBWAA when I assigned seats in the main press box to our local radio and TV sports directors. I'd held 20 seats for them because they had covered the team all season and I didn't feel they should be bounced from their regular season seats. The BBWAA said if those 20 seats were used by radio/TV, we should install a wall to separate them from the writers. I convinced the BBWAA that a wall would block the view of a lot of writers' seats. In the end there was no wall, and the local radio/TV had their regular season seats.

World Series

As was the case with the 1976 All-Star Game, our PR staff was responsible for all media accommodations and a World Series program. This was our chance to show our team and city to the world. Aside from the credentials process, a tremendous amount of detail goes into planning media accommodations from hotel rooms to information kits to hospitality functions to transportation. Bus service was arranged from the hotels to the Vet and back. The last media bus was scheduled for 3 AM after the first night game. I was about to crawl into bed around that time, and the phone rang. It was the PR person assigned to the last bus. There was no bus, and about two dozen media were stranded. Somebody at the bus company screwed up. But the finger pointed at the Phillies—especially me. I called multiple taxi companies, explained my dilemma, and asked if cabs could be sent to the media gate at the Vet ASAP. I quickly dressed and headed for the Vet and had to chauffeur the last five writers in my white Buick station wagon.

* * *

Sparky Anderson once said, "If you lose the World Series, you would still be remembered. If you didn't get there, no one would remember." Boy, we lived that proclamation for three years. Pete Rose had said the World Series would be a piece of cake compared to the NLCS and he was right. The World Series wasn't as gut-wrenching as the Astros series. It was the third World Series in Phillies history. The other two were losses (1915 and 1950).

Leading the series 3–2, we returned home with Steve Carlton on the mound. We felt good about our chances, but it's never over until it's over. After eight innings Chris Wheeler and I headed for our clubhouse, which was to open immediately if we won. Media can enter the clubhouse from the dugout tunnel or the main entrance off the service level concourse. Wheeler was stationed at the tunnel entrance, and I was at the other door, keeping the photographers at bay until the game was over.

A wooden platform was set up in the middle of the clubhouse for the trophy presentation. If we lost the game, all that had to be quickly removed.

The 1980 championship parade concludes at JFK Stadium, which was packed with more than 100,000 fans.

Wheeler and I are watching on a tiny black and white TV monitor on the platform. When Rose caught the ball that popped out of Bob Boone's glove for the second out, I looked at Wheeler. "There's no way we're going to lose now," I told him. We could hear the roar of the crowd when Tug McGraw got the final out. The scar of 1964 tortured generations of Phillies fans until the 1980 team won the world championship. Larry Bowa said it best: "The Ghost of 1964 is dead."

After celebrating on the field, the players began coming in the clubhouse followed by media. It was so crammed, one could hardly move. Schmidt was the MVP. Per Major League Baseball's orders, we had to get Schmidt to the interview room. But by that time, television was already off the air. He was the only World Series MVP who didn't get interviewed on national television up until that point. Schmitty still reminds us about that.

Driving home that morning, I was so elated yet so exhausted. I was so thankful there would not be a Game 7. All that exhaustion went away when Julie and I got to ride in the parade. It was breathtaking to see the masses of millions that lined Center City and Broad Street. Fans were everywhere—even in trees and on top of traffic light poles. The smiles on people's faces will never be forgotten. All the long hours, all the losing seasons, all the rain delays vanished.

To top it off, 100,000 were packed into JFK Stadium for the ceremonies, a scene that was never duplicated. It was a huge love fest. "We Are The Champions" was blaring on the PA system as our floats circled the football field before stopping in the middle of the stadium for ceremonies. Fans were so happy because they, too, were World Series champions. When we got to spring training, Jim Parker, executive director of Clearwater, Florida's chamber of commerce, wanted to salute the world champions with a parade. We had a short one through downtown Clearwater. A crowning moment came on Opening Day in 1981 when we received our World Series rings. The wait and the weight was finally lifted for the Phillies.

Memorable 1980 World Series Moments

Bob Boone "Definitely the parade. To be able to share that with my family was a career highlight."

Larry Bowa "My fondest personal memory is riding in the parade down Broad Street and seeing how the importance of winning affected so many people. All of us—players and fans—were left with memories that we will have forever."

Marty Bystrom "Having the opportunity to start Game 5 of the 1980 World Series in Kansas City. Then a couple of days later, we won the world championship. The parade down Broad Street is yet another tremendous memory."

Steve Carlton "My fondest postseason memory is the parade down Broad Street and interacting with the fans. I was amazed at the number of fans lining the parade route and the outpouring of emotion. It was a combination of joy and relief that the Phillies had won it all."

Dallas Green "Obviously, winning the World Series in 1980 and the mind-boggling parade that followed. I remember standing in the corner of the dugout, arms folded, and taking a deep breath before Tug threw the last pitch. I was never worried that we were going to lose the series, but I wasn't so sure during the gut-wrenching playoffs against Houston."

Greg Gross "The excitement of Game 5 in the 1980 NLCS against Houston and getting to the World Series. The victory parade that followed was another everlasting memory."

Greg Luzinski "Getting two game-winning hits in the Houston NLCS, a homer off Ken Forsch in Game 1, and a pinch-double off Joe Sambito to drive in Pete Rose. As a team, winning the World Series and seeing Tug McGraw strike out Willie Wilson."

Keith Moreland "RBI single in Game 2 of the '80 World Series against the Royals."

Dickie Noles "Winning the World Series in 1980. Just looking around the Vet with Tug on the mound and the excitement of the fans. All players have that dream—bases-loaded, game on the line, and you win the championship. I can still see that moment as though it was yesterday."

Ron Reed "Getting the save in Game 2 of the 1980 World Series is my fondest personal memory from all of the postseasons I participated in. And of course being part of that great Phillies team is a great memory. After getting to the playoffs in 1976, 1977, and 1978, and losing all three playoff series, 1980 was special and a memory I'll always cherish."

Bobby Wine "I remember jumping up and down after Tug struck out Willie Wilson in '80, running on the field, and joining the pile. After the clubhouse scene, I went out to the field to wave to my family because I wanted to share the moment with them. I ran up the tunnel had a beer by myself in the tunnel."

1983

Three years removed from being the world champions, Schmidt and Carlton were among seven players left from that 1980 championship team. Schmitty and Lefty were in their prime. When *Sports Illustrated* called early in spring training wanting to arrange for a cover photograph, I figured it would be for one or both of them. Turns out *SI* wanted Pete Rose, Joe Morgan, and Tony Perez, three members of the Big Red Machine who were now wearing Phillies uniforms. Rose came aboard in 1979, Morgan was acquired in a trade with the San Francisco Giants in December 1982, and Perez signed as a free agent in January of 1983. Interestingly, it was the last season that trio was together. After the season Rose and Morgan were released, and Perez was sold back to the Cincinnati Reds.

Another December trade brought Von Hayes to the Phillies, which sent five players to the Cleveland Indians. Rose immediately nicknamed Hayes "5-for-1." Hayes was the only one in the starting eight under 30 years of age, prompting Stan Hochman of the *Philadelphia Daily News* to label the team the "Wheeze Kids." We brought Morgan and Hayes to Philadelphia for a press conference after the trades. The photo op always includes new players putting on their jerseys and caps. This time the photo op was 5'7" Morgan standing on a ladder to put a cap on the 6'5" Hayes.

There have been some bizarre seasons in Phillies history, and this sure was one. They were inconsistent most of the season and bickered among each other. From Opening Day through August 31, 40 different players appeared in games. With the team in first place (43–42) on July 18, manager Pat Corrales was fired and replaced by Owens, the second time he left the front office for the dugout. In the end the Phillies reached the postseason for the sixth time in the last eight years, but it wasn't easy.

Unafraid of ruffling feathers and benching big name players, Owens took a page out of Green's book. In September Len Matuszek played more games at first base than Rose. Twelve different pitchers made starts, including two rookies, Charles Hudson and Kevin Gross, who combined for 12 wins. The 40-year-old Perez was hitting .391 with 17 RBIs in 19 games on May 1, fitting as it was the 100th anniversary of the Phillies first game.

When September 1 rolled around, the Phillies, Pirates, St. Louis Cardinals, and Expos were separated by two and a half games. The next day Owens used Ozzie Virgil to pinch hit for Morgan, and Virgil hit a game-winning grand slam. On September 5 we were 69–67 and in third place. On September 14 we took over first place for good. With Morgan swinging a hot bat, we won a club-record 22 games in September. That included an 11-game winning streak, a modern club record. Carlton's historic 300th win came during the streak.

The clincher came in a 13–6 win in Wrigley Field 14 days later, and the Phillies finished six games ahead of the Pirates. The win was the 700th in our history. Under Owens, Philadelphia finished 47–30. John Denny became the ace as Carlton had a losing season. Denny went 13–2 after the All-Star Game to finish with 19 wins. At the end of the season, he won the Cy Young Award. When the Phillies had a press conference to commemorate Denny winning the award, we had Denny pose with one of Carlton's awards. Closer Al Holland, who came in the Morgan deal, won another pitching award, earning the Rolaids Relief Man Award by recording a club-record 25 saves.

NLCS

For the third time since 1977, the Los Angeles Dodgers stood in the way of a World Series appearance for us. During the regular season, the Dodgers completely dominated us, winning 11 of 12. That's not all. In those 12 games we scored a total of 15 runs (13 earned). Our team average was .187, and their team ERA was 1.09.

Opening the best-of-five in Dodger Stadium, the Phillies earned a split, winning the first 1–0 on a first-inning Schmidt home run and shutout pitching by Carlton and Holland. Gary Matthews, nicknamed "the Sarge" by Rose, hit a homer in Game 2, our only run in the 4–1 game. The Sarge, who had 10 homers during the season, was just warming up. Homering in each of the next two wins and driving in seven runs, he walked off with the NLCS MVP, and the Phillies won the NL pennant. He keyed an offense that scored 14 runs in its last 15 innings, a total that was one less than the amount of runs scored against the Dodgers during the whole season.

The clubhouse scene after we eliminated the Dodgers was wild. As a PR staff, the main focus was to get players to the TV podium, certainly one of the easiest postgame duties. There wasn't an issue with this group in dealing with the media. So many players had been in the postseason that they knew what to expect.

World Series

The I-95 World Series followed: Philadelphia vs. Baltimore. It was a college reunion for me and Phil Itzoe, now the Orioles traveling secretary. We had dreamed about an Orioles-Phillies World Series in college and now were living it. The series started in Baltimore, and our buses left during the morning for an afternoon workout in Memorial Stadium. I stayed back to finish some details that became stressful. Driving to Baltimore helped calm my nerves, and I decided: no matter what was going to happen going forward I was going to enjoy the World Series and not get stressed out. You never know how many more of these opportunities will come along.

We won the first game and headed home in good shape, tied 1–1 just as we had done in the NLCS. Back at the Vet, the Orioles swept us in three straight to win the series. When Eddie Murray hit the second of his two home runs in Game 5, the clinching game, I noticed Brown was pumping his fists. I barked, "Hey, there's no cheering in the press box."

1983 WORLD SERIES MEMORIES

Kevin Gross "My first full year with the Phillies. As a rookie it was just a great feeling to be part of a team with such great veteran players."

Von Hayes "My fondest memory was celebrating after beating the Dodgers in the playoffs and earning a chance to play in the World Series."

Gary Matthews "Winning the MVP is my individual memory. As a team we were dominated by the Dodgers that season and we got to beat them. I got bragging rights over my friend, Dusty Baker. Advancing to the World Series was special."

Joe Morgan "Bill Giles established a lifelong relationship when I broke in with the Astros and he was the PR man. In 1982 I'm living at home [in Oakland] and playing for the Giants. Giles called me, said he wanted to bring me to Philly to add my leadership to that of Rose and Schmitty. I wasn't sure if I wanted to leave home, but finally Bill convinced me, and I was traded to the Phillies. I struggled most of the year, was hurt a couple of times, but come September I and the team got hot. With me and Garry [Maddox] hitting late home runs, we won the first World Series game in Baltimore but lost the next four. To this day it still bothers me because I know we were the better team."

Ron Reed "It was an unusual season. We must have had six guys over 60 years of age—lots of experience, and it paid off in the end. I had a strange season. I'd come in a game behind by a run or tied. We'd go ahead, and I wound up with a bunch of wins [9–1 in 61 appearances]. Matter of fact, I didn't win another game the rest of my career. Granted, I only had one more season. The last pitch I threw for the Phillies was the last out we got against the Orioles in the series, a grounder to third by Todd Cruz."

Mike Schmidt "It was special for a number of reasons. First, a chance to play with four future Hall of Famers, Rose, Morgan, Perez, and Carlton; second, to go to the World Series with them; third, to watch several young players like Matuszek, Lefebvre, Samuel, Hayes, Diaz, Dernier, and Daulton break into the game and play a role; and last, watch one of the great starting pitching seasons ever, John Denny winning the Cy Young."

1993

The Phillies have had the Whiz Kids (1950), Comeback Kids (1980), and Wheeze Kids (1983). Along came a bunch that had more—and mostly unflattering—nicknames: "throwbacks," "misfits," "rejects," "outlaws," "wild," "crazy." A book about the 1993 team was appropriately titled *Beards, Biceps and Bellies.*

In the end they were the called National League champions and one of the most popular teams in club history. For the first time ever, the Phillies reached three million in attendance. Philadelphia embraces underdogs and blue-collar workers. The '93 bunch was both—except those blue collars were really dirty. During the last-place season of 1992, a year in which clean-cut Dale Murphy was on the team, John Kruk described that team as "24 morons and one Mormon." It's hard to believe that a last-place team could have a nucleus that would produce a championship the next season. Last to first was a first in franchise history.

In spring training a group of 25 different personalities became a team. Some guys didn't like each other, but when they crossed the lines, they went to war as a unit. They had a fight with the Cardinals in spring training and started the season 3–0 in Houston. "I really think that start made everyone believe," Jim Fregosi said.

Offensively, they led the league in at-bats (5,685), runs scored (877), hits (1,555), doubles (297), walks (665), on-base percentage (.351), and total bases (2,422). They just made the enemy pitchers work and work. They had five starters—none homegrown—who won 12 or more games. The closer, Mitch "Wild Thing" Williams, walked 44 in 62 innings but recorded 43 saves. He also got a 10th-inning base hit at 4:40 in the morning to win a game. It was another one of Harry Kalas' great calls: "The game is over! On an RBI hit by Mitchy Pooh!" Nobody ever got another hit at that hour as Major League Baseball changed the rules for when a game could be started. The second game of that July 2 doubleheader began at 1:26 AM. I don't remember what time I left the park, but I do recall getting home as the sun was rising and *The Wilmington News-Journal* was in my driveway.

Five days after the doubleheader marathon, Kevin Stocker was called up to replace Juan Bell at shortstop. Stocker remembers his first game for more reasons than one. The game against the Dodgers went 20 innings before Lenny Dykstra ended it with a double, giving us the 7–6 win. Following one of his at-bats, Stocker went into the dugout tunnel. "Lenny was sitting on a stool, smoking a cigarette," he said. "'You smoke during the game?' Lenny flipped the cigarette on the floor, reached back for chewing tobacco, and put a big wad in his mouth. He looked up and said, 'Welcome to the bigs, kid.'"

We took over first place after Opening Day and never relinquished it. No other Phillies team had ever led on May 1, June 1, July 1, August 1, and September 1. But guess who showed up in September? Yep, that Ghost of 1964. Leading by nine and half games on 9/5, we lost eight of the next 13 games, reducing the pad to four games. Six wins in their next eight games ended it in Pittsburgh on September 28. Seldom used Donn Pall got the last out. Remember that trivia factoid. Kalas' call of the last out was: "Ground ball, it's a fair ball! Kruk to Pall…the Phillies are the '93 National League Eastern Division Champions! This wonderful band of throwback players have won the National League East, mobbing one another on the field." During the club-house celebration—or more accurately, trainer's room celebration—Kalas led the team in singing "High Hopes."

The 1993 team was the toughest to deal with from a PR standpoint. Macho Row at the end of the clubhouse was not exactly *Mister Rogers' Neighborhood*. You had to pick your spots when needing to talk to a player who lockered in that area. The players all squeezed into the trainer's room after home games. They'd rehash the game, get on each other for not busting it or playing the game the right way. Unity is what made that team click. They were 25 players with one goal…and multiple beers.

The clubhouse often would be empty of players and filled with media. If no one surfaced, it was time to enter the den and plead. Daulton saved those of us in PR. "Tell them I have eight more minutes of ice [on the knees]," he said, "and I'll be out." He'd also direct one or two of his teammates back to the clubhouse. You'd approach Dykstra with a request for a live pregame interview on the field in 10 minutes for NBC. He'd answer, "Okay, Dude. I'll be there in 15 minutes or so." *No, Lenny, it's live and in 10 minutes.* Generally, he got there with seconds to spare. Dykstra was a red-light player, meaning when the TV camera was on, he rose to the occasion. He had some kind of a postseason and finished runner-up for the MVP that season.

Kruk was a character, always coming up with some great lines. One of my favorite was: "Lady, I ain't an athlete. I'm a ballplayer." When we had day games after night games, he often slept in the clubhouse. He and the clubhouse kids were known to play Wiffle ball for hours. Yet Kruk probably was the most difficult player I ever had to deal with. Every spring I'd address the team about media cooperation and signing autographs. Did they listen? You probably know the answer. "Baron," Kruk said, "I know you tell us to sign autographs when we get to the park. The same people are there every day. They ain't fans. They are professional autograph dealers. I ain't signing anymore."

Kruk didn't care much for the media either. When you walked into the trainer's room after a game at the Vet, he occupied the first seat on the right. Getting him to vacate his position to go to the clubhouse for the media wasn't easy. The media loved him. He was a character and so quotable. Now he's a media personality on ESPN and a very good one. Just think, three members of this team are now on national television—Kruk, Williams, and Curt Schilling.

Jim Eisenreich, signed as a free agent, led the club in hitting and was one of the many popular players on the club. He had Tourette's Syndrome, a condition that can be embarrassing and troublesome. To help others with the same condition, he made himself available to groups or individuals. He never turned anyone down.

For the first time in 11 seasons, we had three starters—Daulton, Kruk, and Terry Mulholland—in the All-Star Game played in Camden Yards. It almost turned out to just be two. In Fregosi's pregame gathering with the media in his office a couple of days before the All-Star Game, he mentioned that NL manager Bobby Cox named Muholland the starter. Obviously, the media wanted to interview Mulholland who hadn't arrived at the Vet yet. I went outside the clubhouse to alert him. When told he would start, he responded, "I don't want to go to the game. I want the time off to spend with my son." I told him, "Terry, I suggest you go directly to Jim's office before going to your locker where the media is camped out." Fregosi talked him into starting the game.

General manager Lee Thomas (left), manager Jim Fregosi (center), and president Bill Giles celebrate on the field at Veterans Stadium after the Phillies defeated the Atlanta Braves to win the National League pennant in 1993.

That's the same game in which Kruk, batting fourth, struck out against left-hander Randy Johnson in the third inning. The first pitch was a blazing fast ball way over Kruk's head. Next two pitches, he bailed and flailed. "When I stepped in the box, I just wanted to make contact," he said. "After the first pitch, all I wanted to do is live." It still is one of the most amusing moments in All-Star Game history.

NLCS

The experts said the misfits were no match for the Atlanta Braves. They were wrong about this strange best-of-seven series. Kim Batiste, a defensive replacement in Game 1, had a game-tying error in the top of the ninth and a game-winning single in the 10th. Atlanta crushed four homers in a 14–3 romp to tie the series in the next game. The next game was another easy Atlanta win. That 9–4 loss was followed by two one-run wins—real nail-biters—to send the series back to Philadelphia. Veterans Stadium was loud during the playoffs and World Series in 1980. It seemed louder in 1993, especially when Williams struck out Bill Pecota to send us to the World Series against the defending champion Toronto Blue Jays.

Pacing in the clubhouse late in games and not saying a word to anyone was my norm during the postseason. Pitchers who had been in the games were often the only players in the clubhouse. We never made eye contact, let alone spoke. Once in a while, a player, who might pinch hit, would come to the clubhouse and swing a bat, but we still wouldn't make eye contact or small talk. Too much was riding on every pitch. A TV was my connection to what was happening on the field. Once games ended it was time to get ready for the media mass and also time to begin trying to get a couple of players to go to the interview room. Win or lose, the manager was an interview requirement. MLB hoped to have losing players too, but that didn't happen often.

World Series

In spring training the Blue Jays trained in nearby Dunedin, Florida, and it seemed like we played them a thousand times in Pinellas County, Florida. This time we were playing them in front of the world for our fifth World Series and their second straight. Some guy named Pat Gillick was their GM.

A split in the first two World Series games in Toronto brought the series to the Vet. The Blue Jays offense put us in a 3–1 hole with 10–3 and 15–14 wins. Our players were more available postgame during the postseason than during the regular season, which was very helpful. But there was one big exception. That was after Game 4 when we led 14–9 after seven innings only to see the Blue Jays score six in the top of the eighth, a crushing 15–14 defeat. We went 1–2–3 in the eighth and ninth innings, including four strikeouts. It was like Black Friday of 1977—only on a Wednesday. Our clubhouse was totally empty, which was understandable. Fregosi visited the interview room, but getting players out of the trainer's room this time was almost impossible. I don't remember who, but one player finally surfaced and was surrounded by the big media mass.

Schilling then came up with the first shutout in Phillies postseason history to keep us alive as we returned to the SkyDome for the potential two last games. Schilling could be difficult to deal with at times, but he was a clutch pitcher. One time in spring training, I asked him to do a telephone radio interview. "No, and don't give me that tired face of yours," he responded. Little did Schilling realize that God gave me that tired face and a great personality.

An entertaining World Series ended in pain for us. Joe Carter infamously hit a series-ending homer in the bottom of the ninth in Game 6 off Williams. One by one, with heads bowed, our players exited from the dugout and into the clubhouse, which was to open immediately. At the same time, a network TV worker banged his head on a steel beam outside our clubhouse. He was bleeding profusely from his forehead. I ran in the clubhouse, grabbed some towels, and took them to him before he received medical attention.

Williams went to his locker. I decided to wait a few minutes to open the clubhouse. Finally, the media poured in and headed for Williams. He stood there like a man, answered question after question from wave after wave. They were different voices but the same questions. As I was about to rescue Williams, Mulholland took Williams by the arm and led him to the trainer's room. A magical and electrifying season of 97 wins was history. The bunch of misfits couldn't repeat in 1994. Phillies fans were flying high coming off a World Series, but for the second time, a strike pulled the rug from under them.

1993 WORLD SERIES MEMORIES

Larry Andersen "Getting a save in Game 5 of the 1993 NLCS against the Braves."

Darren Daulton "I was exhausted when we clinched the division in 1993 but really proud when we won the pennant. It was sort of a relief knowing we were going to the World Series against Toronto."

Dave Hollins "Beating the Braves in the NLCS and the home run I hit off Greg Maddux in the decisive game. The fan reaction that night is something I will never forget."

Ricky Jordan "Being in the starting lineup as the DH for the first World Series game back in 1993 against Toronto. As far as the fondest team memory, beating the Braves that year."

John Kruk "My fondest personal memory was without question Mitch striking out Bill Pecota at Veterans Stadium to put us in the World Series. I had a great view standing at first base."

Mickey Morandini "Beating the Braves in the NLCS was something I'll never forget. As far as my fondest personal memory, hitting a triple off Greg Maddux to clinch Game 6 at Veterans Stadium. Standing on third base and hearing the Phillies fans make all that noise was quite a thrill."

Mitch Williams "Everybody on the team was on the same end of the rope pulling the same direction all year. I never experienced that on previous teams or any teams after that season."

2008

With Bonnie Clark on board as the vice president of communications, I was still around as an advisor while developing alumni plans. As a rookie I didn't make it to the World Series. She did. Geez, maybe I was the problem all these years.

Fresh from their postseason appearance the previous season, Charlie Manuel's Phillies were expected to be there again in 2008. Bouncing around between first and second the first two months, they took over first place—with the exception of a six-day stretch—on June 1 and stayed there until August 14. Riding second place for all but one of the next 28 days, the Phillies found themselves three and a half games behind the New York Mets. That was the biggest deficit after dropping two of three to the Florida Marlins at home on September 8th, 9th, and 10th.

Then came the Ghost of 1964. Only this time, the Ghost got the Mets. They went 7–10 the rest of the season while the Phillies finished 13–3. The clincher came on a Saturday afternoon at Citizens Bank Park on September 27, the second to last game of the season. Fittingly, Jamie Moyer who had watched the 1980 Phillies as a kid, won the clincher. Clark called me to active duty that day. My job was to keep the third-base photographers from rushing the field after the final out. It was my first time watching an entire game from field level.

Postseason

Julie was diagnosed with chronic obstructive pulmonary disease in spring training and was placed on oxygen. With the aid of a portable concentrator, we were able to be at all postseason games. She and I sat together with our entire family in Hall of Fame Club seats. It was strange not being in the press box anymore, and it was a really tough adjustment, believe me. But unlike that first spring training game in 1964, I now was allowed to cheer. Traveling with the team for road games, Julie and I were fortunate to be included in a private suite provided for some of our owners plus Pat and Doris Gillick and Sylvia and Dallas Green.

Starting in 1994 MLB added a wild-card team, which created an extra round of playoffs. So we were about to experience a potentially a longer postseason. We had to play the Milwaukee Brewers in a best-of-five division series. We won both home games and went to Milwaukee needing one win. That city was buzzing as the Brewers were in the postseason for the first time in 26 years. The Phillies led the league in home runs, and four of them

David Montgomery, Pat Gillick, and mayor Michael A. Nutter took turns hoisting the World Series trophy during the 2008 parade.

produced a 6–2 clinching victory in Game 4. For the second time in nine days, there was a celebration on the field and then in the clubhouse.

Next came the Los Angeles Dodgers in the NLCS. Again, we won the first two games at home and then headed west, needing two more wins. With the largest crowd in Dodger Stadium history, they won the first game in L.A. Matt Stairs delivered the greatest pinch-hit homer in Phillies history, a two-run, game-winner in Game 4. Watching a game from a suite is a lot more nerve-wracking than being in the press box. There I was busy. In the suite, I was nervous. There were times I'd leave the suite and pace the corridor as I couldn't watch. Often, Doris Gillick would also be pacing in the same area. Dodger Stadium brought back the painful postseason memories of losing Game 4 in 1978. But Jimmy Rollins began Game 5 with a home run, and Cole Hamels, Ryan Madson, and Brad Lidge held the Dodgers to one run, and we celebrated in Dodger Stadium this time.

World Series

Clearwater and St. Petersburg rub noses in Florida, they are so close. So a World Series against the Tampa Bay Rays, their first, created plenty of excitement. Games in the domed Tropicana Field were similar to the playoffs in the Astrodome. It was very loud. A split brought us home for the next three games. Games in Philadelphia in late October run a weather risk as there's no dome over Citizens Bank Park. Game 3 was delayed for 91 minutes by rain. Despite hitting three home runs, the game was decided by a swinging bunt that won the game in the bottom of the ninth inning at 1:47 AM. Riding four more home runs, we coasted to a 10–2 win, setting up a possible clincher in Game 5 on October 27. Delaware Valley was on high alert.

Tied at two after five and a half innings, the rain came and stayed. For the first time in World Series history, a game was suspended at 11:10 PM by rain. More rain came October 28, which pushed the resumption back to 8:35 PM on October 29, 46 hours after it was sent into a delay. In a moment that matches McGraw in 1980, Lidge, wearing No. 54, struck out the last batter to clinch the World Series championship. The inverse comparisons are eerie—'80, now '08; No. 45, now No. 54; a left-hander, now a right-hander; McGraw leapt into the air, Lidge fell to his knees. The crowd noise at Citizens Bank Park in October was deafening. We were the first NL team to finish 7–0 in postseason home games, and the Philadelphia fans had something to do with that.

While making plans for a possible on-the-field World Series trophy presentation ceremony, Clark asked if I would get Gillick to the field. He was in his GM box on the press box level, and I was in the nearby Hall of Fame Club level seats when Lidge struck out Eric Hinske. I then made a beeline to Gillick's box. We took the stairway from the press box level to the field. As we're going down the steps, I remember him saying, "I was thinking, one more save, Brad, one more."

Julie and I got to ride in a parade down Broad Street for a second time. I thought the 1980 parade would never be topped, but 2008's journey blew away the first one. The Philadelphia Police Department did a phenomenal job of controlling the jubilant mass of humanity. When we neared Citizens Bank Park, the mass had completely shut off Broad Street. But the police were able to part the sea of red, and we moved on to a celebration at the park. As in 1980, millions of fans lined the parade route, smiling, yelling, applauding, waving, reaching out to touch someone, anyone on the floats. Joy and love were everywhere. Whenever someone on our float raised the World Series trophy, the noise level skyrocketed.

People were everywhere—in trees, leaning out of windows, on ledges, on the City Hall roof. Two men were halfway up the side of a skyscraper, cleaning windows. Children were on the shoulders of parents. Teenagers were on the shoulders of teenagers. It was all races, all ages. Signs were everywhere, too—big, small, professionally printed, handmade. My favorite was: "Mets fans are working today."

Visions of another parade in 2009 ended in New York when the Yankees won the World Series. Sitting on a team bus after losing and seeing giddy Yankees fans celebrating was depressing. Revenge from 1950 didn't happen. More division titles in 2010 and 2011 ensued, but we fell short of the World Series. We've been through that before. Big hopes for 2012 turned into a third-place finish. We were expected to win but didn't—just like in 1979. But five consecutive trips to the postseason is the greatest era in our history, replacing the run of 1976–1983.

CHAPTER 14
NOW PITCHING NUMBER...

Players are often remembered by the uniform number they wore on the back of their jerseys during their playing careers. It wasn't always that way. *Now Batting Number…* by Jack Looney provides a history of uniform numbers and team-by-team rundowns. According to Looney's research, the Cincinnati Red Stockings wore numbers on their sleeves as long ago as 1883. Other reports differed, and verification was difficult to achieve. It is known, however, that when the New York Yankees played in Cleveland on May 13, 1929, it was the first game in which both teams wore uniform numbers. As far as the Phillies, they first wore numbers in 1932. No. 1 that season was center fielder George "Kiddo" Davis. The highest number was No. 30 by right-handed pitcher Ad Liska.

Number Notes

No. 99 is the highest number ever worn by a Phillies player, and it was worn by three players: left-handed pitcher Mitch "Wild Thing" Williams (in 1993), right-handed pitcher Turk Wendell (2001), and second baseman So Taguchi (2008). The lowest is 0, which was worn by outfielder Al Oliver (1984) with 00 being worn by right-handed pitcher Omar Olivares (1995) and right-hander Rick White (2006).

What are the most numbers worn by a player? Two players wore seven different numbers. They were infielder Granny Hamner (1, 2, 6, 17, 29, 33, and 37) and Hall of Fame outfielder Chuck Klein (1, 3, 8, 26, 29, 32, and 36). Shortstop Bobby Wine wore four different numbers in his Phillies career as a player and coach—1, 42, 7, and 13 and then back again to 7. Wine was No. 7 when I joined the team. In 1965 we acquired slugging first baseman Dick Stuart from the Boston Red Sox. He always wore No. 7. He asked John Quinn for it, citing the fact he had always worn that number, he and his wife had jewelry with that number, and his license plate was "7." Quinn called Wine and asked him what number he wanted. Wine said 7, the number he wore in Buffalo in the minors and the number he asked for when he finally made it to the majors for good. Quinn asked again, Bobby said 7 again, and Quinn asked again. "By now, I figured I had lost 7, so I asked for 13. Our daughter was born on the 13th,"Wine explained. "I figured Mr. Quinn would object, but he said okay." Stuart played only one season with the Phillies, and Wine got 7 back again.

Retired Numbers

No. 36 worn by Robin Roberts was retired by the Phillies in 1962. Other retired numbers were 1 (Richie Ashburn in 1979), 32 (Steve Carlton 1989), 20 (Mike Schmidt 1990), and 14 (Jim Bunning 2001). You have to be a Hall of Famer to have your Phillies uniform retired, but policies vary with other Major League Baseball teams. If Curt Schilling, Jim Thome, or Roy Halladay are enshrined in Cooperstown, their numbers will join the Phillies' retired list. In 1997, the 50th anniversary of Jackie Robinson becoming the first African American player, Major League Baseball retired No. 42 on all teams.

Roberts was brought up to the major leagues in June 1948. When he arrived in the Phillies clubhouse in Forbes Field, No. 36 was hanging in his locker. Right-handed pitcher Nick Strincevich wore that number until he was released the day before. As Roberts was getting dressed, Strincevich came up to him and said, "Are you Roberts? Good luck,"When Roberts was sold to the Yankees after the 1961 season, team owner Bob Carpenter said no one would ever wear that number again.

Ashburn wore No. 1 from 1948 through 1959. When he left in 1960, three different players—infielder Alvin Dark, infielder Joe Morgan (not the Hall of Fame second baseman), and Wine—wore that number that season. Carlton wore No. 32 with the St. Louis Cardinals and was given that number with the Phillies. Right-hander Darrell Brandon wore that number the previous season.

Schmidt joined the Phillies in September of 1972 and was No. 22. When Roger Freed was traded that winter, Schmidt was given Freed's No. 20. Bunning was No. 14 in Detroit, so he kept the same number when he came to the Phillies. My hero, Del Ennis, wore that number before Bunning and Pete Rose years later. The Ennis family had campaigned to have No. 14 retired in his honor. They objected when we retired it for Bunning. A fan had also

After announcing his retirement in San Diego in 1989, Mike Schmidt, No. 20, faces the Philadelphia media the next day in a press conference at the home plate of Veterans Stadium.

organized a campaign for Ennis. When Ennis' health was failing, I got a call from a priest asking us to reconsider. Without a doubt Ennis is the greatest Philadelphia native to play for us. His numbers weren't that far off from those of Ralph Kiner, who is in Cooperstown. It was really difficult to say no, believe me. We were also approached to retire 45 after Tug McGraw died. Once again, we stated our policy.

Having one number when you break in the majors and then another one for your career isn't rare. In addition to Schmidt, there was Greg Luzinski. He wore No. 42 in 1970 and No. 19 thereafter. Jimmy Rollins wore No. 29, 6, and 11. Pat Burrell wore No. 33 and 5. Juan Samuel wore No. 9 and 8. Ryan Howard wore No. 12 and 6. Darren Daulton wore No. 29 and 10.

Choosing The Numbers

Who decides what number a player will wear? Generally, it is the responsibility of the equipment manager. When I first started, that was Unk Russell and later Kenny Bush. At times I stuck my nose in the mix. When we acquired Jim Kaat in 1976, he asked for No. 36, which he had always worn. When told it was retired, he asked if Roberts would let him wear it, but we didn't want to go that direction. He switched to 39.

Since Frank Coppenbarger, the director of team travel and clubhouse services, joined the Phillies in 1989 the duties have rested with him. When a veteran joins the Phillies, Coppenbarger will try to give the new player his old number. If it isn't available, Coppenbarger then provides a list of numbers from which the player can choose. When a key player leaves, Coppenbarger will also save that number or put it on ice for a while in respect for that player. He's done that for No. 10 (Daulton), 4 (Lenny Dykstra), 38 (Schilling), 45 (McGraw), 5 (Burrell), and 24 (Mike Lieberthal). "Tim Gradoville wore 38 after Schilling, but he was up for one day and never got in a game," Coppenbarger said. "So officially 38 wasn't worn until 2004 [Tim Worrell]."

Dale Murphy was always No. 3 with the Atlanta Braves. After the Phillies acquired Murphy in a 1990 trade, Coppenbarger thought he deserved to keep that number. Pitching coach Darold Knowles was No. 3. When Coppenbarger explained the situation, Knowles said he understood. So he doubled Knowles' number, making it 33. Turk Wendell came to the Phillies in a 2001 trade with the New York Mets. "He had worn 13, so I gave it to him," Coppenberger said, laughing. "Unfortunately, Turk had about four consecutive bad outings and he asked to switch to 99."

In 2002 Doug Glanville, who had always worn No. 6, returned to the Phillies. Rollins was wearing No. 6. According to Coppenbarger, Rollins volunteered to give 6 back to Glanville, so Rollins became 11. When we acquired Tom Gordon in 2006, he had always worn 36. Coppenbarger explained the situation, and then Gordon requested 45. That number was put on ice after McGraw died in 2004. Since the number hadn't been used for two seasons, Coppenbarger decided to give it to Gordon.

Hunter Pence was No. 9 with the Houston Astros and he wanted that number when he was traded to the Phillies. "Domonic [Brown] had worn that number for over a year, and I just didn't think it was right to take it away from him," Coppenbarger said. "I know Pence was around longer. So I told Hunter. He asked what numbers were available. I said, why don't you wear 3? You'd be the best right fielder to wear that number since Dale Murphy."

It's no surprise what Kruk requested for his uniform number. It wasn't cash. "John Kruk was 19 with the Padres, but we gave him 28. He was fine with it," Coppenbarger said. "Two years later Mitch Williams comes to us, and I gave him 29. Now he wanted 28, so he offered Krukker two cases of Budweiser beer to switch numbers. You know the outcome: Kruk took the beer. Then for some reason, Mitch wanted to switch to 99 in 1993. We went to the World Series that year."

When Ryan Madson was in his first big league camp with the Phillies, he wore No. 63. When he came up to the majors that season, Coppenbarger switched his number. "[No.] 63 was a high number that is more suited for spring training," Coppenbarger said. "So I moved Ryan to 57. After that season he came to me and asked if he could get 63 again. I said, 'Okay, but I'm curious why you want that number.' He said, 'My best friend in high school had a 1963 pickup truck. We rode to school every day in that truck.'"

Switching uniform numbers in season isn't permitted anymore because of Major League Baseball's licensing agreements with manufacturers. If a player wants to change his number, he must notify the equipment manager by July 1, and the change can be made the following season.

ACKNOWLEDGMENTS

Two ownership groups and four presidents in my 50 seasons, unheard of in today's business world. From the Carpenter family to the current group originally formed by Bill Giles in 1981. A presidential parade of Bob, Ruly, Bill, and David. Pretty good continuity.

By contrast, there were 10 different Phillies owners from the first season, 1883, until the Carpenter family stopped the merry-go-round and saved the franchise after the 1943 season. As Richie Ashburn used to say to Harry Kalas, "Hard to believe, Harry."

After the 1972 season, Ruly replaced his dad as the team president. He and I started about the same time in 1963. I kidded him, "Ruly I don't understand. We started the same time. Now you're the president, and I'm still the PR guy." He laughed and said, "Check your blood."

When it all started, I was a one-man band. But as time went on, the department expanded as did the responsibilities.

Thanks to Wheels, Adele MacDonald, Dennis Lehman, Tina Urban, Vince Nauss, Leigh Tobin, Gene Dias, Karen Nocella, Christine Negley, Mary Ann Moyer, Debbie Rinaldi, Greg Casterioto, John Brazer, Scott Palmer, Kevin Gregg, and a flock of interns, including Ed Wade, Kurt Funk, and Scott Brandreth.

We shared a few scars but enjoyed many more laughs.

Also, I extend pity to Debbie Nocito, who has to put up with me in alumni relations.

Special gratitude to Bill Giles and David Montgomery for their guidance, trust, support, faith, and friendship. I was truly blessed to have worked with them. The Phillies are a family because of their leadership.

Then, there are those in the pinstriped uniform, the many members of the media and other employees with whom I rubbed elbows. Thanks to all of them, too.

Not to be forgotten are the fans, millions of them. We share one very important quality, passion for the Phillies.

SOURCES

Books

Allen, Dick; Whitaker, Tim—*Crash: The Life and Times of Dick Allen*; Ticknord & Fields, Boston, 1989.

Bunning, Jim; Dolson, Frank—*Jim Bunning, Baseball and Beyond*; Temple University Press, Philadelphia, 1998.

Giles, Bill; Myers, Doug—*Pouring Six Beers At A Time*; Triumph Books, Chicago, 2009.

Green, Dallas; Maimon, Alan—*The Mouth That Roared*; Triumph Books, Chicago, 2013.

Looney, Jack—*Now Batting Number...*; Black Dog & Leventhal Publishers, Inc., New York, 2006.

Shenk, Larry; Gummer, Scott—*The Phillies: An Extraordinary Tradition*; Insight Editions, San Rafael, CA, 2010.

Westcott, Rich; Bilovsky, Frank—*Phillies Encyclopedia*; Temple University Press, Philadelphia, 2004.

Wheeler, Chris; Gullan, Hal—*View From The Booth*; Camino Books, Philadelphia, 2009.

Periodicals

Phillies Media Guides

Phillies Yearbooks

Phillies Magazines

"After The Game," *Phillies Alumni Newsletter*

The Philadelphia Inquirer

Philadelphia Daily News

Websites

Phillies Insider Blog

phillies.com/alumni

baseballalmanac.com

baseball-reference.com

ESPN.com

National Baseball Hall of Fame and Museum.com

SportsIllustrated.com

ABOUT THE AUTHOR

Left to right: Larry Shenk, Julie, Tyler Shenk, Mike Mosel, Debi Mosel, Audrey Shenk, Andy Shenk, and Renee Shenk.

Larry Shenk
Vice President, Alumni Relations

Larry "Baron" Shenk has been a fixture in the Phillies front office, starting with the 1964 season when he was publicity director. Along the way he became the director of public relations and vice president, public relations in 1981. After 44 years as the head of the Phillies public relations department, Baron assumed a new position with the Phillies in 2008 as vice president, alumni relations.

He has received numerous awards, including the Robert O. Fishel Award (1983) for excellence in the field of public relations; Philadelphia Sports Writers Association Good Guy Award (1995); the Richie Ashburn Special Achievement Award (2003), given to a member of the Phillies organization who has demonstrated loyalty, dedication, and passion for the game; the Dallas Green Special Achievement Award (2007) from the Philadelphia chapter of the Baseball Writers Association of America; and Lifetime Achievement

Awards (2007) from both the Philadelphia chapter of the Public Relations Society of America and the Philadelphia Sports Writers Association. In addition he was inducted into the Central Pennsylvania Hall of Fame (1992) and the City All-Star Chapter of the Pennsylvania Sports Hall of Fame (2004).

Baron has authored hundreds of Phillies publications and is the co-author of *This Date in Philadelphia Phillies History* and *Phillies: An Extraordinary Tradition*. A graduate of Myerstown High School (1956) and Millersville State College (1961), Baron was a general reporter with the *Lebanon Daily News* (1961–63) and a sportswriter with *The Wilmington News-Journal* (1963) before joining the Phillies on October 23, 1963.